Wholehearted
Teaching
of Gifted Young Women

Wholehearted
Teaching
of Gifted Young Women

Cultivating Courage,
Connection,
and Self-Care
in Schools

Kathryn Fishman-Weaver, Ph.D.

PRUFROCK
PRESS INC.™

PRUFROCK
ACADEMIC
PRESS

A line of materials supporting scholarship and research-based practices in education

Library of Congress catalog information currently on file with the publisher.

Copyright ©2018, Prufrock Press Inc.

Edited by Stephanie McCauley

Cover and layout design by Allegra Denbo
Cover image *Masked* by Sara Rose Ashbaugh

ISBN-13: 978-1-61821-818-6

Printed in the United States of America.

At the time of this book's publication, all facts and figures cited are the most current available. All telephone numbers, addresses, and website URLs are accurate and active. All publications, organizations, websites, and other resources exist as described in the book, and all have been verified. The authors and Prufrock Press Inc. make no warranty or guarantee concerning the information and materials given out by organizations or content found at websites, and we are not responsible for any changes that occur after this book's publication. If you find an error, please contact Prufrock Press Inc.

Prufrock Press Inc.
P.O. Box 8813
Waco, TX 76714-8813
Phone: (800) 998-2208
Fax: (800) 240-0333
http://www.prufrock.com

Dedication

This book is dedicated to the young women whose personal stories and wisdom guided this project. I have tremendous hope for the world they and their peers will lead.

Table of Contents

Table of Contents

List of Figures

Acknowledgments

First and foremost, this book would not have been possible without the wisdom, guidance, and enthusiasm of the student researchers. It gives me great hope to know they are contributing their ideas and positive energy to different college communities and professional fields around the globe. Our world is a better place because of the courage, compassion, and creativity of young people like these.

My family members are the greatest champions of my work. My husband, Christopher Fishman-Weaver, often took on the lion's share of childcare and housework so that that I could research, write, and teach more. He's not only read every chapter of this book; he's also read every iteration of each chapter. Along the way, he's encouraged me with editing notes and an endless supply of dark chocolate. Our children, James and Lilah, inspire me to keep working for more wholehearted schools. They are proud to introduce me as Dr. Fishman-Weaver and sometimes announce to random strangers at the grocery store, "Our mom is writing an important book." My parents, Gloria and Lenny Fishman, raised my sister Kelsey and me to believe we could do anything we set our minds to do. That lesson has inspired the way I teach, lead, and live.

When I moved into school administration, I had no idea that I would have the privilege to fall gracefully (or, often, not so gracefully) into my very own "empowerment group." Stephanie Walter, Maria Isabel Morandi, and Katherine Sasser have all been the willing recipients of endless text messages about education, gender, learning, and grammar. We frequently cook together in my kitchen, and lean on one another for support. Their friendship has left its mark on this book and also on me as a human being.

As much of this research and writing was part of my dissertation, I would be remiss not to thank my brilliant committee and professors. Dr. Jeni Hart is a wonderful feminist mentor to me professionally and personally. We still meet for coffee so I can badger her with countless questions, proposals, and quandaries. These meetings mean more to me than she could possibly know. In addition to her maven copyediting skills, Dr. Emily Crawford encouraged and guided my writing and research throughout my Ph.D. program. You would be hard-pressed to find more thoughtful or encouraging professors than my two other committee members, Dr. Ty-Ron Douglas and Dr. Lenny Sanchez. Finally, Dr. Jen Clifton—one of the most well-read people I've ever met—first taught me about participatory action research. It was her class and her ongoing recommended reading lists that put me on this research path.

I have Marilyn Toalson to thank for getting me into my professional role in gifted education—what a treat for your favorite middle school teacher to later become your teacher mentor. The following school counselors offered wise and patient guidance to the students in our empowerment groups and also to me: Matt Miltenberg, Betsy Jones, Leslie Kersha, Melissa Coil, and Jane Piester. Jill Clingan and Chris Holmes are two of the most talented writers and teachers of writing that I know. Their insights, edits, and encouragement helped make this manuscript stronger.

Finally, I would like to thank Stephanie McCauley and the good people at Prufrock Academic Press for believing in this project and nurturing it to publication. Like teaching, writing a book is a community project.

PART I

A Case for Affective Education

This is the story of 20 women. It is a story of courage, connection, and self-care. The soundtrack for our story is the sweet cacophony of high school and college: laughing, weeping, wailing marching band instruments, cheering at athletic events, and the syncopating ding of Facebook and text messages received. In the background you can almost hear our mothers; they speak to us in quick Mandarin, Vietnamese, English, and Sinhalese. Of course, this is also my story. There are signs of this work everywhere. My desk, for example, is cluttered with snapshots of student groups. Along my basement wall are stacks of journals and binders of notes that stand as tall as my 6-year-old. I pause, remembering advocacy projects, counseling groups, meals shared, and successes celebrated. I consider how my experiences as a teacher led to this research, but how once I began researching, I realized that my experiences as a student led to my teaching. So much of this is cyclical. This is a story I have been waiting to share.

The gifted and high-achieving young women I worked with have the intellectual capacity and emotional sensitivity to make significant advancements in their respective fields (Lubinski, Benbow, & Kell, 2014). However, there is trepidation surrounding their bright futures (Robinson & Reis, 2016). They face great pressure and often insufficient social-emotional support (Kerr, 1994; Kerr & Foley Nicpon, 2003). Further, the messages they receive about gender continue to limit the ways they experience college and career (American Association of University Women, 2018; Bell, McLaughlin, & Sequeira, 2002; Clance & Imes, 1978; Kerr, 1994; Kerr & Foley Nicpon, 2003; Miller, 2014). My research explores how 20 young women negotiated these messages and experiences in high school and college, and how educators can use these lessons to employ more wholehearted strategies in schools.

As usual, I am getting ahead of myself. . . .

Let's back up and start again, this time in a high school classroom at lunchtime. The teacher (me) is optimistic and naive. The room is packed with students. If an administrator dropped in, she would probably comment on how messy (and warm) the room is. Papers, art materials, and lunch trays line the tables and counters. Students sit, sometimes two to a chair. A group of juniors crowds around my desk eating the cheese crackers I brought for my own lunch. I don't know yet that over the next several years these students will change the way I teach, lead, and parent. A few minutes later, the bell rings and students scatter, racing off to class. For a moment the room is quiet. I look around and shake my head, gathering up the homework students left when they hurried out. I throw away a few abandoned milk cartons. I sit down to finish my Diet Coke and wonder what the rest of the day will bring. Just then a young woman walks in, almost in tears.

CHAPTER 1

The Masked
Affective Crisis

Title

Masked

Artist

Sara Rose Ashbaugh (2014), senior in high school

Artist Notes

 Masked has a dual meaning; it expresses both the pressure I feel from society to achieve perfection, and the reluctance I sometimes have to speak. My original idea for the project focused on the pressure that I and most women feel to wear makeup every day. For me, makeup has become a crutch, something to hide behind, and if I leave the house not wearing any I feel naked and exposed. It is a way to hide any imperfections I feel ashamed of. As I worked on the project, it developed another meaning for me. Often, in a large group of people (especially people I don't know) I find myself passively sitting on the sidelines, watching rather than participating. My fear of being judged negatively by others for what I say and do sometimes cripples me, and I find myself doing nothing at all. Masking the girl's mouth in this piece became an expression of my own self-doubt.

"What Is Your Central Story?"

I love to ask students about their central story. They often look at me with surprise. No one has asked them before. They consider the question for a few moments and then start telling me a story. A central story is a quandary you play over and over in your head. If asked, most of us have one or two big questions or experiences we are carrying, wrestling with, and need the space to explore. Stories are critical sensemaking tools. Melissa's central story was about her complicated relationship with her mother. Faith's was her recovery from anorexia. Leslie's was about the role self-doubt played across her experiences. Claudia's explored what it meant to her to be a woman scientist. Elaine's was about the ways her different identities intersected to make her uniquely Elaine.

These central stories were critical tethers in our group dialogues. As we shared our lived experiences, we began to place courage, connection, and self-care in the context of our own narratives. Story sharing was an act of both empathy and connection; in listening to each other's stories, we saw our own lived experiences (Appadurai, 2006; Heron & Reason, 2001; Morrell, 2004). Because of the longitudinal nature of this study, I had the privilege of seeing how central stories shift over time, how new chapters are written and how conflicts resolve. Sometimes stories are also left unfinished, placed on the shelf for later review, while new narratives beg to be explored.

This book is the result of listening to and analyzing many central stories shared by gifted and high-achieving young women. This book is also the result of my story as a teacher, a researcher, and a high-achieving woman. During this project, our multiple narratives crossed, informed one another, and often led to surprising plot twists. Personal stories are the shortest distance between people. They were also the heart of this project. The setting for many of the stories shared in the following pages was a red-bricked suburban high school in the Midwest.

School Context

It is a college town like many others in the central United States. You wouldn't have any problem finding an ice cream shop, pizza parlor, or church. In the summer everyone talks about how hot it is while children eat sticky popsicles and chase fireflies. In the fall the leaves turn orange and gold. Friday night means high school football. Saturdays are for college football. In the winter everyone talks about how cold it is, and the kids turn their pajamas inside out, hoping to increase their chances of a snow day. In the spring the trees blossom, and we take long walks on the soggy trails. People who move away come back because it really is "a nice place to raise a family." Of course, this town has nuance as well, sweet bits of character that make it special to the 100,000 people who call this particular place home.

This town houses three major postsecondary institutions, including a flagship university. Education is the lifeblood of the community. The university and colleges host rich cultural arts events. Extensive bike and hiking trails line the community and surrounding areas. There are four public high schools and three private high schools in town. Community support for schools is strong. Other top industries in the community include healthcare and insurance.

Barnwood Academy[1], the focus high school, opened its doors in the 1970s as the second public high school in town. At the time, it was significantly smaller than the other high school and was surrounded by farmland. Given suburban sprawl and growth, the school is now in a densely populated community with restaurants, shops, and businesses. Since opening, the high school has doubled in physical size and quadrupled to more than 2,000 students, making it the largest high school in the community. The school's student ethnicity demographics are 71% Caucasian, 12% African American, 6% Asian, 5% Multiple, 5% Hispanic, and less than 1% Native American. Barnwood's vision and commitment statements emphasize shared decision making, collaboration, and a focus on student learning. The school operates on a block schedule and allows juniors and seniors open campus privileges throughout the day. Barnwood has a robust Advanced Placement (AP) program with 19 AP courses across all subject areas. The orchestra, band, debate team, and journalism programs earn state and national titles regularly. During our research, the school was also experiencing tremendous success in athletics, with 20 state championship titles over the course of a few years. Seventy-five percent of students go on to 4-year institutions after high school.

During this project, I served as the division chair for the gifted program at Barnwood. The gifted program was considered a model in the state. Teachers who wanted to start or improve their own high school gifted programs frequently came to observe at Barnwood. The heart of the program

---

1 The information for this section was gathered from the institutional website for the focus high school. It is not cited here to preserve the confidentiality of the research site.

was an open-door resource room. Open door meant that any students who wanted to participate in our programs or services were welcome, whether or not they had been formally identified as "gifted." Our instructional team hoped that this open-door practice would increase access and participation of students of color and students in poverty, who are underrepresented in traditional gifted programs (Ford & Grantham, 2003). Although we did see encouraging gains in diversity as a result of this practice, the majority of students in the gifted program were White and Asian. Barnwood's gifted program had many program partners, including the guidance department, community internship hosts, and several service-learning sites.

Discovering the Masked Affective Crisis

When I became the division chair for the gifted program at Barnwood, the previous chair shared that our most pressing issue involved a group of eight young women who were just starting their junior year of high school. She confided that they were struggling with a host of social-emotional challenges. These were straight-A students who took advantage of our robust AP program. It was common for them to take six AP courses a year. Most of the young women also played two instruments, studied advanced levels of one or more world languages, and competed in various science, technology, engineering, and mathematics (STEM) events. Because of these impressive activities, the faculty considered the young women to be excelling students. Hence, the teachers and administrators were caught off guard when these "successful" students began presenting with a host of alarming social-emotional challenges evidenced from depression, including suicide ideation, anxiety, disordered eating, and unhealthy relationships. Shortly before I joined the department, several of these issues reached crisis levels that required outside agency intervention from psychologists, doctors, and even the juvenile system. As the new educational leader for our department, I had to do some creative problem solving—and fast. I went to my mentors in gifted education. I went to the literature. I partnered with our school's comprehensive guidance department and later joined their professional learning community (DuFour, DuFour, & Eaker, 2008). I met with students, parents, and mental health professionals. I was desperate to better understand the nature of what I came to call the *masked affective crisis.*

In response, our gifted education team started an "empowerment group" for these gifted young women. Over the years, this empowerment group became a cornerstone in our gifted education department and the foundation for my work on affective education. Although the students in our inaugural group were extraordinarily high-achieving, they were often plagued by self-doubt. They shared that they did not always think of themselves as smart, that they were reluctant to speak up in class, and that they worried about their ability to get into competitive colleges and to experience success after graduation. In that first year, our questions were practical and hyper-local in nature: What were the immediate mental health needs of this student group, and how could we address them?

Working with educational leaders from the guidance and gifted departments, we coached students on strategies for leading more balanced lives. These strategies included forming a peer group, volunteering, and practicing mindfulness and gratitude. We encouraged the young women to schedule in fun, and when they resisted, saying they "didn't have time," we added just-for-fun activities to our meetings and shared research with them on the benefits of laughter. These empowerment group meetings sparked powerfully reflective conversations and important lasting relationships. Although the social-emotional needs (and, in some cases, scars) would never go away completely, after a few months of our group, we noticed a healing process beginning.

Once our students were in a safer place, I was able to step back and explore this masked affective crisis more deeply. How had we missed it? How could we prevent another similar affective crisis?

As this project evolved into a research study, I looked at the issue from a broader academic vantage point. There are striking patterns among what we had seen at Barnwood and what the research reported on the unique social-emotional needs of academically high-achieving young women (Kerr, 1994; Maurer, 2011; Rimm 1999). Gifted young women are often absent from educators' schemas of potentially vulnerable populations. We seldom think of valedictorians as "at-risk" students (Lovecky, 2011). I believe this masked issue in schools is the consequence of a hyper-focus on achievement and complicated hegemonic notions of gender and success (Amen & Reglin, 1992; Robbins, 2006). Although often cast as the "winners" in an educational game, high-achieving young women continue to present with many alarming affective needs, including depression, anxiety, disordered eating, and unhealthy peer or romantic relationships (Di Cintio, 2015; Fiedler, 1999; Kerr, 1994; Lovecky, 2011; Robbins, 2006). In fact, this casting as extraordinarily successful may exacerbate both the problem and our schools' failure to address it. These social-emotional patterns represent dual issues. First, gifted and high-achieving individuals present with different affective developmental patterns than their peers. Second, and relatedly, schools rarely have structures in place to proactively respond to and/or nurture the needs of these high-achieving learners. Gross (2002) cited lack of intentional peer groups as the primary mismatch between school and the needs of gifted learners. Gross contended that this mismatch between the nature of gifted learners and the school environment is more important than any fundamental differences between gifted learners and their average-IQ peers. This means that with more intentionality around peer grouping[2] and community, schools could better nurture the needs of gifted learners and make a significant positive difference.

The political pressures for standardization and academic accountability experienced by administrators, teachers, and students are prime examples of a hegemonic achievement structure (Beyer, 2002; Ferguson, 2006; Reis, 1987; Waite, Boone, & McGhee, 2014). Of course, we want students to do well, to be challenged, and to learn throughout their school career (and beyond). Holding students accountable for learning and teachers accountable for teaching is certainly not a system of oppression in itself. However, when accountability structures are set up to systematically privilege certain groups of students and types of achievements over other groups of students or qualities of excellence, then that system can become problematic. Within recent school reform movements, accountability and standardization have been used as a hierarchical system to designate who is valued and who is not (Lipman, 2003, 2004; Mathison & Ross, 2002), and why they are or are not valued. Research has shown that overachievement and standardization are seen as normative in schools (Ferguson, 2006; Mathison & Ross, 2002; Robbins, 2006; Waite et al., 2014). Affective needs are often seen, at best, as auxiliary to academic needs and, at worst, as irrelevant to standardized and high-stakes curriculum (Colangelo, 2003; Lovecky, 2011; National Association for Gifted Children [NAGC], 2014).

There are many troubling consequences of such a system. The one I focus on is how the "hegemony of accountability" in high schools masks affective needs in general, and the affective needs of high-achieving students in particular (Mathison & Ross, 2002, p. 88). The students I worked with asked important questions about the relationship between stress,

---

2 In small and rural schools, setting up like-peer groups can be more complicated, as the number of students in gifted and high-achieving programs may be extremely small. Possible solutions include reconstructing peer groups around related identities or other common interests/experiences and connecting students to enrichment programs off-site or through online platforms.

achievement, the high-stakes culture of schools (Mathison & Ross, 2002; Robbins, 2006; Waite et. al., 2014), and their own social-emotional well-being (Ferguson, 2006; Lovecky, 2011). These questions were consistent with counseling trends for gifted students, which include support in peer relationships, emotional and social adjustment, and stress management (Moon, 2002).

The inaugural empowerment group taught me how educators, counselors, and parents could better support the affective needs of academically high-achieving young women on the precipice of college. Some of the strategies, such as storytelling, building community, and practicing disclosure, surprised me. As a researcher, I attempted to better understand the conditions that had contributed to that first masked affective crisis, as well as our ability to intervene and remediate similar crises in the years that followed.

Seven years after that first empowerment group, I am still in contact with many of the young women from our groups. Several are now in graduate programs, working in industry, and starting law and medical school. They call and message me with news about their latest adventures. They send book recommendations and questions about applying for graduate school or fellowships. They stop by my house and office during winter or summer break to visit over coffee, borrow books, and talk to my daughter about science. I am grateful for these insights and the friendships I have developed with these women over the years.

Following our empowerment group, several of the students continued to work with me on a longitudinal study around the masked affective crisis. We used a participatory action research model. (For more information on the model that guided my study, see the Methodology Appendix.) Through reflective journals and interviews spanning 5 years, the student researchers shared their experiences coming of age during the transition from high school to college. These personal stories shape both the narrative structure of this book and my deeper understanding of the masked affective crisis. As a writer and language arts teacher, I encouraged the use of storytelling and writing for both inquiry and activism. The student researchers and I kept two-way and group journals throughout our study. Several of these journal excerpts are included in this book, such as the following one by Leslie.

LESLIE'S JOURNAL
Senior in High School

January 17, 2015

God, I'm so tired. I submitted five scholarship applications this week, and I still have more due for February 1st. Just the thought of more work makes me even more tired. I just don't want to do anymore work. I'm so stressed, I want to cry. No, correction: I am crying, for no reason in particular, of course. I'm crying for everything, for the walls that I feel are closing in on me. I know that graduating from high school and going to college is supposed to liberate you, but it doesn't feel that way. I feel like I have to go to college, to fulfill my parents' wishes and society's norms. And I want to go to college, that's the thing. I know that I will learn a lot, meet new people, and that it is the only way I can have success in my future life. So yes, college is a good thing. College will be a good thing but it doesn't seem like that now. It seems like the only reason I'm not happy and that I've gained weight and that I don't get enough sleep and that I fight with my mom and that I am becoming apathetic towards my classes and that I am currently crying. And other people just don't seem to understand that. Other people think I have it sooooo easy, that I'm smart so it will ensure my success in the future. But they're wrong, I know that. I have to work hard to get the things I want: the grades, the scholarship money, the college acceptances. Just like football players have to practice to win games, I have to do my work to get better at doing future work. My mom always tells me "to those whom much is given, much is expected." If that's not a blatant pressure, I don't know what is . . . yet I know she only means the best and that she's given so much work in the college process too and supported me tenfold. But sometimes it doesn't seem that way. Sometimes we get in all-out screaming matches. I don't know what to do most of the time. I just take it one day at a time, trying to focus on the small tasks at hand. That's the only way I can cope with all this stress.

Another stress factor in my life: boyfriend. This is my first real boyfriend and it was supposed to be the fun part of my senior year and someone who I could always turn to for support. It started out that way, for the first two months. But things hardly ever turn out the way we want them to. I feel like I am putting more effort into our relationship that [sic] he is and that he just doesn't care as much as I do. And ugh. There is never enough communication. He doesn't text me enough and I'm too chicken to actually tell him I'm unhappy. And I think to myself: would I be better off if I broke up with him? No, certainly not. I like him too much. But I need to stop stressing about him and our relationship. I need to stop. It needs to get better. But I just don't know how. AHHHHHHHHHHHH!

Another stress factor in my life: not enough alone time. I am an introvert. I used to come home from school and have the house to myself for a few hours. I got to be alone. And then my dad lost his job and so he is always at home. Always. And so I don't find peace there. And I can't find that peace at school, because all the people. And when I'm not at school or home, I am usually doing some extracurricular activity or doing college/scholarship apps at my mom's office. And I can't drive so I can't go find myself somewhere else. And many times it's too cold to go walking to my favorite quiet bench spot under a tree. The only time I'm alone is when I'm sleeping, and even then I have dreams that haunt me when I wake up. I am maxed to my limit. I need my space but people keep asking me to do more and more things for them and of course, I can't tell them no. I need to find myself again. I need to be alone.

Another stress factor in my life: the future. WHAT DO I DO AFTER HIGH SCHOOL? I DON'T KNOW HOW TO BE ANYTHING OTHER THAN A HIGH SCHOOL STUDENT. MY WHOLE LIFE, I'VE BEEN PREPARING TO GET MYSELF INTO COLLEGE. AND I'M SCARED. I'm scared I won't be successful or it won't be how I imagined it. I'm scared I'll never learn how to drive and that I'll be a horrible adult. God, I'm so scared of the future. And now I'm crying again.

Although I am a researcher and now an educational administrator, I think of myself as a mother and teacher first. My interest in health, wellness, and the social-emotional needs of high-achieving young women began not in theory, but in practice, with students I care about. This work concerning affective needs for high-achieving young women has struck a chord with other gifted education personnel and parents. I have been asked to write and lecture on our empowerment groups at gifted education conferences across the state and nation. After my presentations, there is always a group of teachers and parents who thank me for addressing their students' or daughters' experiences. One of these people will often take me by the arm and lead me to another gifted coordinator, counselor, or parent, saying that my session sounded "just like" the young woman or group of young women they "were worried about." I listen to the accounts of so many young women who remind me of the students I care for and work with: bright, talented, intense students whose needs are unnoticed or misunderstood and, therefore, often unaddressed.

The young women from our empowerment groups told me they experienced rhetoric from educators and educational leaders that went something like, "She has a 4.0/is in a gifted program/is an AP student, so she must also be doing well socially and emotionally." Young women in gifted and advanced programs are often considered academic superstars (Kerr & Foley Nicpon, 2003; Kindlon, 2006). However, this "stardom" has an unintended consequence—superstars are generally considered to be thriving, and, therefore, it is too easy to miss their struggles. There is a tendency among educators to falsely relate quantitative measures, such as ACT scores or GPA, to qualitative measures of health and well-being (Kerr & Foley Nicpon, 2003). In organizational theory, what I call *the masked affective crisis* is known as an organizational blind spot (Bolman & Deal, 2013). Bolman and Deal posited that when faced with ambiguous data, people fill the gaps with information they do have, or have seen, regardless of whether or not that information is true. For example, I often observe educators dismissing the affective needs of academically successful young women by not selecting them for counseling or social-emotional groups and by failing to recognize their affective challenges until they present in crisis level (e.g., the advanced stages of an eating disorder or suicidal thoughts). The students I worked with wanted to offer a counter and critique to these kinds of narratives. Together we wanted to venture new ways to improve affective supports for academically high-achieving young women.

Why Women?

I focused on young women in particular because I observed firsthand how gendered pressures caused high-achieving young women to experience school in ways that complicated and called into question key aspects of their identities, including, but not limited to, being high achievers, athletes, leaders, and/or scholars in STEM fields (Kerr, 1994; Maurer, 2011; Will, 2015). Achievement trends in school have long shifted so that young women now outperform young men (Kerr & Foley Nicpon, 2003; Kindlon, 2006). Regretfully, even as bright girls and young women achieve at high levels in school, they face different pressures and barriers than young men.

These pressures include traditional feminine archetypes, such as beauty, sexualization, passivity, and domesticity (Wiseman, 2009). Additionally, young women frequently feel pressure to have "perfect" social, academic, and personal lives—an impossible quest that some scholars have called "superwoman syndrome" (Miller, 2014). Our student research teams attempted to sort through these gendered complications. In doing so, we learned that although there are patterns such as those listed previously, gendered experiences are, in short, difficult to generalize. We left with a more nuanced and messy understanding of what it means to be a gifted young woman, as well as more compassion for young men in gifted and advanced programs.

Giftedness: A Loaded Label

Giftedness is a loaded label. It is associated with privilege and tracking (Renzulli, 2011). Intentionality concerning the labels and terms we choose to use or not use is important to me as a researcher and an educator. Implicit (and explicit) bias in tracking, referral, and identification processes all contribute to a lack of diversity in gifted programs. Identification processes often require a referral, and teachers are less likely to refer students from traditionally underrepresented groups (Fishman-Weaver, 2015). African American, Hispanic, and low-income students continue to be underrepresented in gifted education programs (Ford & Grantham, 2003; Renzulli, 2011).

During my work in gifted education at Barnwood, I attempted to problematize and respond to systems that sometimes excluded very bright students from gifted programs. To this end, we ran our department as an equal-opportunity or open-door program, meaning there were no prerequisites to participate, such as earning a specific score on an IQ test (Fishman-Weaver, 2015). We did this because gifted education has important historical and social connotations that map to specific systems of privilege and advantage, particularly across race and class lines (Ford & Grantham, 2003).

I often draw on literature from the gifted education canon. In drawing on these scholars' work I use the term *gifted*. However, the term *high-achieving* is more inclusive and closer to what I am trying to encapsulate with regard to the stressful nature of the high-stakes school environments the student researchers navigated. The term is also more aligned with the literature on talent development, which suggests that achievement and giftedness are malleable depending on social-emotional conditions (Neihart,

2016; Subotnik, Worrell, & Olszewski-Kubilius, 2016). For this reason, I often refer to the students in this study as *high-achieving*. I recognize that all of these terms are imperfect: The term *gifted* has left out too many groups of people, and the term *high-achieving* often negates affective needs. Therefore, I do my best to reconceptualize these terms through the stories of the young women in this research.

Academic Achievement

Academic achievement was both meaningful to the students on our research teams and relevant to high-stakes schools (Hoy, Tarter, & Hoy, 2006; Mathison & Ross, 2002; Robbins, 2006). In high schools, achievement is measured by GPA and test scores. The student researchers were invested in keeping these quantitative measures as high as possible (Hoy et al., 2006). However, these quantitative indicators tell only part of the story of a student's lived experiences, passions, and accomplishments. The young women I worked with wanted to expand definitions of achievement to include more categories, such as music, athletics, and service (Dweck, 2006). As a teacher and researcher, I want to identify a wide range of work that stretches young people's cognitive and affective development. We don't yet have enough formal structures in school to recognize the different ways young people are learning and making a difference.

These tensions between achievement and well-being contribute to specific, albeit often unaddressed, social-emotional concerns for gifted and high-achieving young women (Colangelo, 2003; Di Cintio, 2015; Ferguson, 2006; Kerr & Foley Nicpon, 2003; Maurer, 2011). The "gifted" and "high-achieving" labels don't help with this issue. Calling an individual "gifted" may mask the unique challenges that high-achieving and high-IQ individuals encounter, including sensitivity and overexcitability (Lovecky, 2011). According to Di Cintio (2015), "To speak of giftedness as a disability seems counterintuitive. Part of the problem may be simply semantic; the word 'gifted' suggests an advantage and does not conjure up the intense challenges these children can face" (para. 15). Our research aimed to unmask and help us better understand the lived experiences of academically high-achieving young women during high school and college. It is my hope that educational leaders and stakeholders will use this deeper understanding to put in place new supports for students, teachers, and counselors, including policies, programs, and professional development.

Crisis as a Call to Action

In K–12 schools, the primary onus to safeguard and nurture students' well-being rests in the hands of teachers, counselors, and parents (Kerr, 1994; Kerr & Foley Nicpon, 2003; Rimm, 1999). Barbara Kerr (1994) wrote,

> The implications for gifted girls and women of the data at our disposal are great. We know from other studies . . . that the conditions of adolescence in our society . . . [point] to the awesome responsibility teachers and parents have to protect and promote the self-esteem and aspirations of gifted girls. (p. 168)

Sylvia Rimm (1999) echoed Kerr's (1994) position that adult stakeholders have the potential to support gifted and high-achieving young women through their struggles. Although this is challenging work in our over-achievement and patriarchal culture, Rimm (1999) wrote, "It is possible for you to set high expectations for your daughters [or students] and build their confidence without placing debilitating pressure on them" (p. 53). We wanted to test this proposition.

I was personally inspired by the vulnerability, creativity, and thoughtfulness of the young women in our groups. Their emotional disclosure as they worked through challenging situations that included disordered eating, unhealthy relationships, anxiety, and depression taught me important lessons on courage. These lessons continue to influence how I teach, lead, and parent. Further, these insights directly informed the framework for Wholehearted Teaching covered in Part III.

Through my work, I refer to a social-emotional phenomenon I called the masked affective crisis. I chose the term *crisis* for three reasons. First, I believe it is necessary to disrupt the hushed way we speak (or do not speak) about affective needs. By addressing social-emotional concerns directly, educational leaders can offer wholehearted tools to help students navigate these challenges. Calling a crisis what it is helps us to better understand the gravity of situations that are happening in our schools and to respond proactively. Second, throughout my teaching practice, I repeatedly saw issues reach such critical levels that they needed outside agency intervention, including mental health, medical, or juvenile services. Most of the students in my inaugural empowerment group were in crisis when I took over the gifted department. Third, I know that if these issues continue to go unaddressed, they have the potential to rob high-achieving young women of their complex, rich, and multilayered selves (Lovecky, 2011; Maurer, 2011). This last point about the tumultuous nature of gifted potential is a relatively new theme in the research on gifted youth (Robinson & Reis, 2016). The research on talent development suggests that giftedness: (1) is closely linked to social-emotional skills, (2) requires deliberate development and practice, and (3) can be lost if neglected (Neihart, 2016; Subotnik et al., 2016). Using the term *crisis* signals the urgency of this issue.

EVE'S JOURNAL
Junior in College

October 14, 2014

Being back in college after a year on medical leave is really freakin' challenging. After being self-isolated for a year, jumping back into a social life is quite shocking—especially when I'm expected to socialize a lot within my scholarship program. I've found I lack the confidence and perhaps even the interpersonal skills to effectively make friends. I never feel like I belong. I always leave a conversation with regrets and feeling like I gave off the wrong impression. I don't know how to not hate everything. These difficulties have resulted in increased anxiety and depression and A LOT more solo TV watching.

Balance is challenging for me. I find it extremely difficult to balance my eating, socializing, and family. This is a constant challenge that I will face for the rest of my life, especially because it is a hallmark of borderline personality disorder.

. . . In all honesty I fear that being gifted has made my college experience a little more difficult. I think A LOT. A ridiculous amount. My mind is constantly going a mile a minute. Because of this, I've rarely had to work super hard. So now I'm faced with copious amounts of work that I just don't want to do. I'd rather think. I get really really frustrated because we sit there learning about some obscure opinion but none of it really matters. I feel like I'm wasting my time. Not that I don't enjoy some of the curriculum, I certainly do. And I love my professors. But a lot of the time I feel like I'm wading through for no reason at all. The concepts and even facts are easy for me to grasp but I have no motivation to put in the effort to do the actual assignments. I DO do them, but it's a bit of a battle. I need to work on my long-term goals, now that I plan to live long enough to achieve some. I think it will help my motivation.

Yes, *crisis* is a strong word, so I want to spend a moment disrupting the notion of being in crisis. The students I work with, like all young people, are wonderfully complex. Even as they struggle with intense social-emotional challenges, they are brilliant, compassionate, and creative (Lovecky, 2011). I recognize that *crisis* can be a trigger word and have noticed uncomfortable reactions when I share this work with other academics. Part of my agenda as a teacher-researcher is to disrupt the definitions and structures that limit our capacity to understand young women's experiences. *Crisis* is one of these terms. Each year, as I formed research and empowerment groups with young women, we added other concepts to disrupt, including *strength, vulnerability, courage, achievement, self-care,* and *self-harm.*

These concepts often took on deeper meanings when they were challenged or seen within the context of crisis. Some of the crises the students experienced were products of systems of inequality, including sexism, heterosexism, and racism. Our research teams supported work to end all systems of inequality. Challenging hegemonic systems of advantage and disadvantage could lead to fewer crises, particularly those due to bullying, violence, and discrimination. This is a noble pursuit, and I believe student leadership could be a powerful force in bringing about this change. However, it would not be possible, or even beneficial, to eradicate all crisis experiences. As I worked with the students in this book, I came to see how being in crisis is integral to our lived experiences. Tensions, challenges, and heartbreak are part of coming of age; students need adults who acknowledge these difficulties and help young people find the tools to navigate them. Although I have learned to view crisis as part of the human condition, I do not advocate complacency in the face of any of these situations. In fact, I advocate just the opposite—direct and compassionate action.

Wholehearted Living

We used Brené Brown's (2010, 2012, 2015) work on wholehearted living as a conceptual framework for our study. Wholehearted living is the process of engaging in vulnerability, sensemaking, courage, compassion, and connection from a place of worthiness (Brown, 2010, 2015). As discussed previously, those who practice wholehearted living are not immune to crises:

> [T]hey don't have better or easier lives, they don't have fewer struggles with addiction or depression, and they haven't survived fewer traumas or bankruptcies or divorces, but in the midst of all of these struggles, they have developed practices that enable them to hold on to the belief that they are worthy of love, belonging and even joy. (Brown, 2012, p. 105)

Wholehearted living gave me a conceptual framework to think through potential supports for students to develop resilience to crisis and challenge during times of transitions. Although our research focused on the transition from high school to college, the more the student researchers and I learned about crisis, affective education, and wholehearted living, the more we realized that these skills are transferable across other challenges.

Vulnerability and Storytelling

Vulnerability includes honest disclosure to oneself and others. In order to make sense of our personal and vulnerable experiences, we relied on storytelling and story sharing. Through a partnership with Making Waves, a youth radio program, several of the student researchers were able to learn more about storytelling and then practice public literacy. The students who participated in this project created and shared personally charged and vulnerable stories through our local NPR member station. Many of the stories shared during our research had not been shared before, and some were deeply embedded in feelings of shame. Brown (2010) wrote that shame is a masked issue in society, much like the affective crisis described in this chapter. Therefore, practicing wholehearted living requires a kind of unmasking: "We realize that to live with courage, purpose, and connection . . . we must again be vulnerable. We must take off the armor, put down the weapons, show up, and let ourselves be seen" (Brown, 2012, p. 112), or in the case of our students' radio work, let ourselves be heard.

Self-Compassion and Perfectionism

Self-compassion is the practice of treating yourself with kindness and care. This is a delicate issue with high-achieving young women, who find that perfectionism is reinforced by schools, parents, and even their peers (Rimm, 1999). Perfectionism has been cited as a primary counseling focus for gifted and high-achieving young people (Schuler, 2002). High-stakes pressure and stress in schools can reinforce perfectionism by encouraging students to connect their self-worth to the grades and scores they receive: "So rather than questioning the faulty logic of perfectionism, we become more entrenched in our quest to live, look and do everything just right" (Brown, 2010, p. 57). This maladaptive relationship between perfectionism, achievement, and self-care was one our research team sought to untangle (Neumeister, 2016). We wondered how we might marry academic achievement and self-compassion to create a new culture of courage, creativity, and wellness in our schools.

Teacher as Researcher

Teaching is not a profession; it is a lifestyle grounded in relationship building. Real relationships cannot be compartmentalized into a Monday through Friday, 8:00 a.m. to 3:30 p.m. schedule. Instead, teaching relationships include near constant planning, worrying, instructing, listening, discussing, researching, grading, and counseling. In this way, being a teacher is not merely what you do; it is an essential part of who you are. Throughout our research, I drew on my background, training, and experience in teaching and leading diverse student populations. I have taught in urban and suburban schools in gifted education, general education, and special education. Across all of these settings I've found that relationships are the heart of great teaching.

In my experiences in schools, a small percentage of students often requires a significant percentage of emotional and administrative energy. When I worked in gifted education, this group was almost always our highest-achieving young women. These students had my cell number and e-mail. They shared essays with me over Google Drive. They texted me their good news and worries, both of which were decorated with a creative array of emoji. These messages lit up my nightstand. Over time, these people became the student voices in my head. Their narratives informed my teaching, planning, and understanding of the youth culture in our school gifted program.

Although I know it was impossible to remove all power dynamics inherent in the teacher-to-student relationships, I attempted to engage in transformative (Kezar, Carducci, & Contreras-McGavin, 2006; Shields, 2004) and feminist teaching practices (Belenky, Clinchy, Goldberg, & Tarule, 1997) that build learning communities instead of hierarchies. In my teacher role, I had the privilege of crafting a professional position that put relationship building at the center of my work. Students and I frequently talked over tea or took long walks on campus. I coached students through their course planning, connected them to internships in their areas of interest, and coordinated service projects around the issues they were passionate about. I edited personal college essays. I met with families to set high school and postsecondary goals. Students spent their free time studying and socializing in my classroom. We puzzled over complex math problems and played board games together. There was an annex to my classroom that once served as a small office. My students nicknamed this space "the crying room," as we used it to talk through difficult issues: anxiety, stress, arguments with parents and friends, and college and scholarship rejections. The room lived up to its namesake as we went through a lot of tissues.

Telling Our Story

The student researchers and I examined how identities are conceptualized through language (e.g., the term *gifted* or *woman in STEM*), who espouses such messages (e.g., the media, teachers, counselors), and for whom they speak (e.g., self or others). This critical sensemaking allowed us to untangle the messages, narratives, and stories that mattered to us. By design, our research teams did not include any adult leaders except for me. In an effort to understand youth culture and student experiences, I wanted to work with young people. I sought out the perspectives and voices of young people as they were experiencing the masked affective crisis (Belsey, 2002; Collins, 2000; Elliott, 1991; hooks, 2000; Maguire, 1987; McIntyre, 2008; Morrell, 2004). Their stories offer enthusiastic, complex, counter-hegemonic[3] narratives about what it means to be an academically high-achieving young woman.

---

3 *Counterhegemonic* refers to contradicting, complicating, or speaking back to the dominant or status quo opinion.

Throughout these chapters, I am proud to share many excerpts and vignettes from the students in their own words. This nonlinear, multivoiced structure is aligned with the work of scholars invested in humanizing research (Charmaz, 2014; Irizarry & Brown, 2014; Kinloch & San Pedro, 2014). Kinloch and San Pedro referred to this type of narrative structure as

> a framework for telling, retelling, and re-presenting stories in nonlinear ways—from left to right or right to left. Such nonlinearity leads us to present stories in ways that appear messy, complicated, complex, and multi-voiced, which is why we rely on storying. (p. 22)

By purposefully montaging these stories, I hope to give you the cozy feeling of taking a spot on the couch in the Women's Center, or a beanbag in my classroom. I invite you to settle in and hear the warm, complicated, animated dialogues of students talking to (and occasionally over) each other.

MY JOURNAL
Kathryn

May 31, 2015

I pull up to our church at exactly 2:00 p.m. The parking lot is full. Faith's recital starts at 2:00 p.m., which means I am running late, again. Luckily, it is my church, too, and I know my way around. I tiptoe back to the sanctuary and hear the most exquisite piano music. Today is Faith's senior recital: an hour of piano and voice by her. I slide in next to our pastor, who is running the soundboard. After the first song I move a little closer to Faith.

She alternates between quick and complex piano music and sad, difficult vocals. She is magnificent. She wears a floor-length purple gown. I see her mother in the front row. I recognize that nervous look and notice that she is holding her breath. She must know each spot that Faith has struggled with. Periodically she lets out a sigh of relief after a triumphant note or measure. Two rows in front of me is another set of parents that

21

I have worked closely with. Their daughter is also in Faith's grade and spends a lot of time in my classroom.

Because the people immediately in front of me are very tall, I have to crane my neck to see Faith. This means for most of the recital I listen while watching her between two familiar sets of parents. I think about all of the conversations I have had with these families over the past few years. I think about crisis. Both families have contacted me when their daughters were in crisis. As I look back and forth between these two families and listen to Faith's melancholy and powerful vocals, I wonder if crisis isn't much more common than we usually think. I wonder if there are some unavoidable scars of adolescence. I wonder if teachers could reimagine these crisis moments as learning opportunities. I wonder if we couldn't re-envision challenges as part of the human condition.

Faith has one song that is different from all of the others. It is in English, and the chorus says, "I am not afraid of anything." It is my favorite piece she performs that day. After the recital I talk to Faith's mom. She thanks me for my support. I congratulate her on her daughter. There is an understanding between us as mothers. It is something special, hard to define, almost palpable. We embrace.

Later Faith and I pose for a photo in the sanctuary. As we smile for the camera, one of Faith's classmates comes up to congratulate her. I turn to leave, but am caught by his question, "Faith, I noticed all the songs you sang were so sad. Are you okay?" Faith does the same thing I've caught myself doing in similar situations—she laughs.

The moment passes.

A Note About Pronouns

I conducted this research *with* (as opposed to *on*) teams of bright young women. Participatory, critical, and feminist methodologies are central to my research agenda. Therefore, many of our decisions, presentations, and activist projects were done collaboratively. When this was this case, I refer to the work as *our work*. However, as the facilitator and author of this larger study, there were times when I made decisions on my own. These decisions ranged from choices about methodology, design, literature review, longitudinal analyses, and much of the broader storytelling about this work. In these cases, I use the pronoun *I* to let the reader know that this is a part of the project I directed or authored. Regardless of pronouns, all aspects of the project were vetted by student research teams to the extent that they were interested and available to do so. Consistent with our youth participatory action research (YPAR) and feminist commitments, the chapters in this book are directly informed by the stories and dialogues of our research community. For more information on YPAR, please see the Methodology Appendix.

CHAPTER 2
The Precipice

Title
The Precipice

Artist
Maddy Mueller (2014), senior in high school

Artist Notes
Fists clenched, shoulders back, chest puffed, wind blowing through her hair, ready to go!! That's how I feel half the time about college and the other half I'm looking off the edge in terror.

In the spring of 2014, our student research team hosted an art event called "Perspectives on the Precipice." At the event, the students showcased their original art pieces exploring themes of stress, identity, and mental health. They also gave a presentation to educational stakeholders and parents on their social-emotional experiences during the college application and decision process. Several of their images from this project are shared throughout the book. The following are a few notes from the evening of our art opening.

MY JOURNAL
Kathryn

April 2014

The student researchers are exhausted. It is Monday after a huge weekend. In the last 72 hours they've had a track meet, the Relay for Life all-night walkathon, the art department art show, prom, and a major AP Biology test. Tonight is our art opening and presentation.

Jana and I leave school a few minutes early and drive to the bagel shop to start setting up for the event. Mel pulls up a few minutes later to help. She is usually self-conscious of her height and so I am glad to see her confidently walk into the restaurant wearing heels. Sasha drops off Belle on her way home to change and pick up her art. Ashley and her boyfriend pull up next. Everyone is hungry. I rummage through my work bag and find some granola bars and dried fruit for the students to snack on.

Sasha returns and immediately busies herself arranging and straightening everyone's artist statements. She tells me she is starving. I find some clementines and chocolate in my work bag.

This is the first art event the bagel shop has ever hosted. In a couple hours the students transform the familiar bakery into a gallery and performance space.

At 6:00 p.m. parents and teachers start arriving. They are followed by school counselors, a retired gifted teacher, the activities director, and our principal. A few minutes later the varsity track group runs in—literally.

They are here for Jana. They compliment her art, enjoy a few cupcakes, and jog off as a group.

Two professors from the university arrive, both accompanied by classes of graduate students. The student researchers are poised and confident. They answer questions about our research methodology, process, and the aims of our study. I hug the professors and thank them for their support. The director of the Women and Gender Studies department snaps a photo of our research team for their department Facebook page. A sociology instructor asks if we will present this project to his undergraduate lecture class.

At 7:00 p.m. we start our formal presentation. The students explain that our study explored the stresses of college planning, high achievement, and coming-of-age. To introduce our themes, Mel performs a song. A few bars into her performance, she stumbles, forgetting the words. "Oh shoot!" She laughs. Unfazed, she restarts, confident and powerful. The room is startled by her talent, which feels bigger than this small bagel shop. Next, the students define feminism and youth participatory action research (YPAR). The students lead the presentation, explaining our findings and answering questions.

At the end they ask if I will share a few takeaways. I tell the audience that through this project "we learned that educators, counselors, and teachers absolutely must do more to support the social-emotional needs of gifted and advanced students, especially during senior year. All of the stages of the college applications and decisions process are wrought with feelings of judgment, fear, and apprehension. However, within this tumultuous period are also important moments of hope and strength. Sometimes it is easy to miss these good things. We all need to find ways to engage in those positive moments, to celebrate our students' strengths, ideas, and the adults they are becoming."

Several parents and counselors nod.

The Precipice: Navigating the Space Between High School and College

The student researchers referred to the transition from high school to college as a *precipice*, a term that was solidified after our art showcase and continued to evolve throughout our study. By situating extra attention on the senior year of high school and the period immediately following graduation, we were able to explore a complex period of coming-of-age and identity development. At present, the U.S. educational system is marked by a sharp disconnect between K–12 and higher education (Amen & Reglin, 1992; Boyer, 1986; Lee, Dickson, Conley, & Holmbeck, 2014). K–12 and higher education are seen as separate and distinct entities; I believe we need more work to smooth that sharp divide (Amen & Reglin, 1992; Lee et al., 2014). The college transition is a particularly tough time to maintain supportive relationships. In addition to their trusted peer group, new college students may lose contact with the high school teachers and counselors with whom they have built rapport during their formative adolescent years (Fishman-Weaver, 2014).

During this research, I conducted two focus groups with students in the critical months preceding high school graduation and leaving for college. For many high-achieving young people, senior year is marked by emotionally intense experiences and conversations with parents, family members, and peers. In their research on college choice, Myers and Myers (2012) found that these family conversations were an important factor in determining which school a student ultimately attended. During our team meetings, the students and I often processed these and other intense conversations together. The students knew our classroom was a safe space to bring their unedited concerns, and they trusted that I would be there to listen and, when needed, connect them with other adults in our school who could support them during the complexities of senior year.

This support network matters. However, the research suggests that once students leave for college, they may also leave behind these kinds of social support systems. In their large sample (1,118 participants) longitudinal study of the transition from high school to college, Lee et al. (2014) found that "the transition to college can be a stressful experience, and may initiate or exacerbate depressive symptoms in emerging adults" (p. 560). Many of the students in this research project were already struggling with depressive symptoms in high school, which made me concerned about how these issues might manifest in college.

Overachievement Culture

Pressures in school often stem from academic demands; however, students also experience pressures from peer, family, and extracurricular influences (Rimm, 1999; Robbins, 2006). Some pressure is essential (and even important) in education—we grow through challenge. Our study tried to identify the tipping point between healthy pressure and unhealthy pressure. Amen and Reglin (1992) conducted a study of stress factors for high school seniors. The literature they drew on suggested that academic emphasis and stress can be positive factors if applied *in moderation*; however, this same stress and academic emphasis "can be detrimental if applied *in excess* [emphasis added]" (p. 27). Their research suggests that stress in schools, particularly for high school seniors who are coming of adult age and making difficult choices about their postsecondary paths, is an important concern for teachers and counselors. College decisions are wrought with emotion, and because gifted students are already noted for their emotional intensity, senior year can be a particularly challenging period between childhood and independence (Lovecky, 2011; Kerr, 1994; Maurer, 2011).

Hoy et al. (2006) wrote of school environments that have an academic emphasis. Academic emphasis in schools is characterized by

> the extent to which a school is driven by a quest for academic excellence—a press for academic achievement. High but achievable academic goals are set for students; the learning environment is orderly and serious; students are motivated to work hard; and students respect academic achievement. (p. 427)

What are the emotional consequences of academic emphasis in schools, particularly for young women? Is it possible for schools to have too much academic emphasis? Alexandra Robbins (2006), a mental health advocate and investigative journalist, argued that yes, schools—particularly high schools—often suffer from too much academic emphasis. In her study of high-achieving students, she characterized the high-stakes, high-stress environment of schools as an "overachievement culture." Robbins found that mental health concerns, including suicidality, were a product of the high-stakes school environment:

> In 2003, 16.5 percent of high school students made a suicide plan, and nearly 9 percent attempted to follow through with it. Among college students, one study found that one in four had considered suicide. A variety of factors contribute to student suicides, but there is no doubt that overachiever culture also plays a significant role. (p. 357)

Moreover, long-term school stress has been linked to depression, drug use, ulcers, asthma, eczema, hives, headaches, arthritis, hypertension, colitis, and heart disease (Amen & Reglin, 1992). This is a serious issue with both social-emotional and physical consequences.

Overachievement and perfectionism may be self-perpetuating for gifted and high-achieving young women who find that these traits are often positively reinforced by educational leaders, parents, and even peers (Neumeister, 2016; Rimm, 1999). Therefore, addressing perfectionism with high-achieving students is challenging. As Rimm (1999) wrote, "It is difficult to help an internally pressured girl to back off from her overstudy. Her overstudy and perfectionism have made her so successful . . . for working too hard" (pp. 128–129). The students in our empowerment groups were experiencing a critical time when myriad pressures (including those mentioned previously) often came to a head. How can schools better support the affective needs of their students in light of this intense academic pressure?

MY JOURNAL
Kathryn

December 2013

Text from Tara: I GOT IN, SO MUCH WEIGHT OFF MY CHEST AHHHH!

Tara is talking about a highly selective college. She was so stressed about college decisions coming out today that she started crying while we were talking earlier. Unlike the other students on our research teams, I'd never seen Tara appear rattled by the stressors of high school or the college applications process. We sat together in the bright colored chairs in the gifted room and I listened as she told me about her fears and worries.

At the end of our conversation, she told me her mom was making ribs for dinner, her favorite. "Well, tonight we are having ribs, so they'll either be celebration ribs, or they'll be just ribs."

Tara promised she would text me the news either way, but she said she was "hoping to send a text all in capital letters." I look at her message again and smile. Tara's first choice school was the same as that of several of her classmates this year. So far, I've only heard from Tara. I wonder about the other students who applied.

I type a response: "Oh my goodness! I am so happy for you, Tara. I am also very proud of you. :) :) :) Enjoy those celebration ribs with your family. I can't wait to celebrate together soon."

An hour later she texts me again. She is out with two of my students who applied to the same school and weren't accepted. They are all having ice cream. She tells me she is lucky to have such great friends.

Affective Development: A Brief Overview

Educational psychologists Krathwohl (2002) and Nuhfer (2005) wrote of two primary domains, a cognitive domain (thinking) and an affective domain (feeling). Our study explored the possibilities for stronger affective programs in schools. Affective education includes supports for students' personal, social, and moral development. This section gives a brief overview of the major theories undergirding affective education. Throughout this study, I read widely across educational, sociological, psychological, psychoanalytic, and neuroscientific sources to gain a more rounded understanding of the history and field of affective education.

Affective (or sometimes *moral*) needs include feelings, emotions, motivations, and personal and social development (Ferguson, 2006; Gilligan, 1982; Gilligan, Ward, Taylor, & Bardige, 1988; Hoge & Renzulli, 1993; Lee et al., 2014; NAGC, 2014). Several psychological and educational theorists have built on the concept of affective education to better understand students' emotions, motivations, and behaviors. The following theories are traditionally cited as contributing to affective education: Maslow's hierarchy of needs, Kohlberg's stages of moral development, Bloom's taxonomy of learning, and Krathwohl's affective taxonomy in response to Bloom (Ferguson, 2006).

Maslow's, Bloom's, Krathwohl's, and Kohlberg's theories are all described in the following paragraphs. However, feminist and other social theorists took issue with the linear, masculine, and hierarchical nature of these theories (Gilligan, 1982). They suggested that human behavior and motivation is not linear or always hierarchically ordered, but instead may be circular. For example, the needs Maslow described are indeed human needs, but they are only possible through relatedness (Hanley & Abell, 2002), social connection, and collaboration. Feminist scholars, including Belenky et al. (1997), Brown (2010, 2012), and Gilligan (1982; Gilligan et al., 1998), whose works are cited in this chapter, built on the vital importance of relationships, interdependence, and social networks in their theories. These constructs became critical components in our research team's work around affective education.

Maslow (1970a, 1970b/1964), a psychologist, argued that human behavior and motivation were hierarchical, meaning that people's needs must be fulfilled in the following order: physiological, safety/security, belongingness and love, esteem, cognitive, aesthetic, and self-actualization and self-transcendence. This list reflects Maslow's last version of the hierarchy, in which he also accounted for higher order needs, including beauty, potential, and service (Huitt, 2007). Benjamin Bloom (1956), an educator, put forth a taxonomy that included the following hierarchy of thinking tasks: knowledge, comprehension, application, analysis, synthesis, and evaluation. Krathwohl, an educational psychologist, aimed to provide a schema that built on Bloom's work while also accounting for the intersection and interaction between the affective and cognitive domains (Krathwohl, Bloom, & Masia, 1964). His affective taxonomy outlines stages of internalization whereby people can apply learning to behavior.

Kohlberg (1981), a psychology professor, proposed that all people move through three levels of moral development. Level one is characterized by pre-conventional/pre-moral orientations toward punishment and ego. Level two is characterized by conventional/role conformity where moral choices are determined by perceptions of "being good" and following authority or the social order. Level three is characterized by post-conventional principles where moral choices are determined by conscience and principles of right and wrong.

Although scholarship on the affective domain was dominated by men's voices (Gilligan, 1982), feminist and women scholars offered important critiques and responses to these traditional affective theories. Scholars, including Carol Gilligan (1982; Gilligan et al., 1988), Deirdre Lovecky (2011), and Mary Belenky et al. (1997), offered and/or continue to offer meaningful insights into the affective domain in general, and the psychological development of women (and in the case of Lovecky, high-achieving women) in particular.

Carol Gilligan worked as a research assistant for Kohlberg (Blum, 1988). Although both scholars were invested in moral development, Gilligan criticized Kohlberg's insistence that advanced moral development was always characterized by impartiality and rationality. Instead, Gilligan suggested that moral development is particularized, especially for women. In her language, there is "a different voice" in moral development; this "female voice" (her term) includes historical context, relationships, and an ethic of care (Gilligan, 1982). Gilligan (1982) published her critique of Kohlberg, *In a Different Voice*, to much acclaim. In this volume she posited her theory on moral development. This work opened new conversations around both ethic of care and women's psychological and moral development:

> The truth of the women's perspective to the conception of moral development is to recognize for both sexes the importance throughout life of the connection between self and other, the universality of the need for compassion and care. (p. 98)

By insisting that compassion, care, and relationships are salient factors in moral decision making, Gilligan (1982) was able to offer "a more generative view of human life" in the conceptualization of moral development (p. 174). In 1988, Gilligan and her colleagues published *Mapping the Moral Domain*, a volume of articles expanding the theoretical base of *In a Different Voice*.

Belenky et al. (1997) continued to offer new insights into knowing, relationships, and development in their seminal work *Women's Ways of Knowing*. These ways of knowing include silence (as a schema for disadvantage), received knowing (learning through listening), subjective knowing (containing the largest group of participants in the sample, representing a shift from the previous ways of knowing to beginning to assume personal agency), procedural knowing (characterized by constant analysis and reason), and constructed knowing (an integration of rational and emotional knowledge beginning in metacognition). The participants in Belenky et al.'s study conceptualized constructed knowing as an

> effort to reclaim the self by attempting to integrate knowledge they felt intuitively was personally important with knowledge they had learned from others. They told of weaving together the strands of rational and emotive thought and integrating objective and subjective knowing. (p. 134)

The book, now in its 10th edition, concludes with the educational implications for these ways of knowing as they play out in the context of families and schools, including the complex relationships of daughters with fathers and mothers, discourse patterns as manifestations of power, and the need for classrooms that take into account women's ways of knowing and that empower women students through affirmation and high expectations.

Across all of the theories mentioned in this section is the notion of journey. Development is always a journey. Our research suggests that although there are certain patterns we can anticipate across these journeys, each person's path is uniquely contextualized, dynamic, and often nonlinear. Teachers have the privilege and responsibility to walk with students through important development years in their affective and cognitive journeys. Affective education explores the tenuous, albeit symbiotic, relationship between social-emotional and cognitive needs. If left unaddressed, these social-emotional needs, particularly in gifted and young women populations, can lead to the affective crisis (Fiedler, 1999; Lovecky, 2011, Robbins, 2006). Our research groups worked to develop a healthier framework to support affective development. This framework for Wholehearted Teaching is explained in detail in Chapter 6.

Gifted Education and Affective Development

Many scholars in gifted education (Hoge & Renzulli, 1993; Kerr, 1994; Kerr & Foley Nicpon, 2003; Lee et al., 2014; Lovecky, 2011; Rimm, 1999) have suggested that high-IQ individuals present with more intense affective needs than their average-IQ peers. The intensities of gifted individuals translate into intense social-emotional particularities, vulnerabilities, and needs (Colangelo, 2003; Kerr, 1994; Lovecky, 2011; Rimm, 1999).

To address their unique social-emotional needs, gifted and high-achieving learners require different interventions and supports than their average-IQ and average-achieving peers. Positive disintegration, to use Dabrowski's (1964) term, can be a more intense process for high-IQ students. Dabrowski (1964, 1967, 1970), a psychiatrist, posited that personality and sense of self are developed through a process of disintegration (changes in self-concept). Positive disintegrations push individuals to develop increased sensitivity toward altruism and morality (Mendaglio, 2002). Disintegration can be a painfully emotional process but tends to lead to a more developed self-concept. Dabrowski also explored overexcitability in gifted and high-achieving populations. Overexcitability (OE) refers to highly sensitive responsiveness to stimuli and is a common topic in the literature on gifted populations (Lovecky, 2011; Mendaglio, 2002). The validity of OE as a psychological construct associated with giftedness is currently under some scrutiny (Vyuk, Krieshok, & Kerr, 2016). However, we do know that gifted youth present with a deep openness to experience and that this openness is often misinterpreted (Amend, 2009) or in mismatch with the structures of school.

In her study of 92 gifted individuals, Deidre Lovecky (2011), a psychotherapist, identified five traits often inherent to a gifted child's identity. She said that these traits—divergent thinking ability, excitability, sensitivity, perceptiveness, and entelechy (known roughly as self-determination)—can contribute to "social-emotional vulnerability" (p. 1). However, the behavioral manifestations of these traits vary considerably according to psychological and social factors, some of which are within a child's (or adult's) locus of control, and others that are innate to the individual. The following points explain these specific psychological and social factors (Lovecky, 2011):

› *Divergent thinking* is characterized by a preference for the creative, unusual, and original. It often presents in youth as absentmindedness and disorganization.

› *Excitability* is characterized by high energy, emotional reactivity, and high arousal of the central nervous system. Excitable students are often "stimulus seekers," or children with a "need for novelty" (p. 4). They tend to experience powerfully intense emotions.

› *Sensitivity* is characterized by a strong depth of feeling, including passion, compassion, and empathy. Sensitive students intensely commit to people and ideas. They can be overwhelmed by strong feelings. It is sometimes difficult for a sensitive person to distinguish between her own feelings and the feelings of those around her.

> *Perceptiveness* is characterized by an ability to understand multiple aspects of a situation simultaneously and to arrive quickly at the core of an issue. Perceptive students often have a strong commitment to truth, fairness, and justice. They are haunted by guilt when classrooms, schools, or society do not exhibit the ideals of truth, fairness, and justice.

> *Entelechy* is characterized by self-determination, goal setting, and inner strength. The strong will of students with entelechy is often misinterpreted. Students with entelechy have a tendency to take on too much responsibility and struggle to set appropriate limits. For example, a strong-willed young person may constantly berate her teacher for not recycling her soda cans and consequently develop a tense relationship with her.

Gender adds yet another layer of complication in understanding the social-emotional needs of high-achieving young women navigating the transition from high school to college: "There are special issues for gifted girls, such as decreased self-esteem, at-risk behaviors (eating disorders, substance abuse, and unsafe sex), inequity in the classroom, and the culture of romance" (Kerr & Foley Nicpon, 2003, p. 502). Barbara Kerr's (1994) research on "smart girls" explored why bright young women who receive high grades and high test scores continue to lose confidence throughout their school experiences. Isolation and loneliness are common feelings among high-achieving young women in high school (Rimm, 1999, p. 13). Yet these feelings become overshadowed by high-achieving students' academic success (Ferguson, 2006; Lovecky, 2011), which creates the conditions for the masked affective crisis. As a result, counselors and gifted education personnel too often end up responding retroactively to social-emotional issues, risky behaviors, or the unrealized potential of high-achieving young women.

These struggles are particular to the intersection of gender and giftedness (Kerr, 1994; Maurer, 2011; Rimm, 1999), yet they are mostly absent from the educational literature on vulnerable populations. Ginny Maurer (2011), a gifted educational scholar wrote, "Although growing up a girl is just plain hard . . . growing up a gifted girl with an intense degree of perfectionism, perseverance, sensitivity, empathy, nonconformity, or introversion, may make it even harder" (p. 198). Likewise, the transition period from high school to college presents students with significant affective challenges (Amen &

36

Reglin, 1992; Fishman-Weaver, 2014; Lee et al., 2014). Our research team explored some of the ways gender and high achievement interacted during the transition between high school and college. We used affective education to explore healthier solutions for positively nurturing and managing the social-emotional traits outlined previously. Creativity, compassion, courage, energy, and higher order thinking can all be positive traits, particularly when they are nurtured with appropriate social-emotional supports. This study begins to fill the gap between literature and practice in understanding and addressing the affective needs of high-achieving young women.

Intersectionality and Coming-of-Age

We all brought multiple identities to this project; at various times, certain identities were more salient than others. We used an intersectional analysis to better understand how these different identities worked both in concert and tension with each other. *Intersectionality* is a structural analysis and critique of systems of social identities and inequalities (Collins, 2000; Crenshaw, 1989; Grzanka, 2014). It is an active attempt to complicate and add multidimensionality (Crenshaw, 1989) to the theorizing of identity (Nash, 2008). Kimberle Crenshaw (1989, 1991), a feminist scholar, first introduced intersectionality into the literature in her work around Black women in critical legal studies (Ferguson, 2006; Grzanka, 2014). Through sharing our lived experiences and interrogating our own positionalities, our research teams explored race, class, gender, sexual orientation, age, nationality, and other identities (Collins, 2000, 2013; hooks, 2000; Snyder, 2008).

Gender was one social identity within a milieu of multiple salient identities for each of the student researchers. We paid attention to the ways gender intersected with other identities, particularly race/ethnicity and cognitive ability. Additionally, we discussed the ways age, socioeconomic status, and sexual orientation influenced the varied experiences of the student researchers. Cultural and social identities contributed to complex advantages and disadvantages during the tumultuous period just before leaving for college.

Navigating these identities was messy and complex. For example, the student researchers spoke of how they took issue with mainstream gender norms even as they actively strove to "fit in" with those same norms. We used intersectionality to bring our different interests, experiences, and identities into a broader scholarly discussion of power (Zack, 2005). Through sharing our lived experiences, we were able to engage in a counterhegemonic process of unraveling dominant storylines.

EXCERPT FROM ELAINE'S COLLEGE ESSAY
Senior in High School

Fall 2015

At a young age, my parents each escaped a war-ravaged country on a fishing boat, leaving their parents, in hopes of finding a world that would allow them the freedom to live their dreams. Despite their hardships and struggles, they persevered; both becoming the first in their families to earn a college education—my mother a successful entrepreneur and my father a respected nuclear engineer. This success[,] however, did not define them to the extent . . . their selflessness did, having sponsored 23 of their relatives. In this sponsorship, my father has said, "I have given them the pole. Now they have to catch the fish." . . . They have given me a sense of family they never had; they have instilled a sense of community and compassion never shown to them, and they have done all of this without expecting anything in return. This is pride, this is dedication, and this is love.

To simply match their passion would be an accomplishment in and of itself; but I know there is more, as I have always sensed incompleteness. My parents have shown me the path of living a comfortable life. . . . While they have established a solid foundation on which our family was built, it is up to me to expand upon it. . . . Unlike my parents, I have been given a stable family life; a solid support system and an inherent understanding of unconditional love. I have been given a fishing pole, one that I will hold fast to, no matter how hard life tugs. I am a proud second generation Vietnamese-American, casting my line in the sea of life.

Theoretical Framework: Feminism

Gender was important in how we experienced ourselves as embodied individuals, how we interacted with others, and how we contributed to the production of knowledge (Butler, 1990, 2015; Crotty, 1998). Although identifying as a girl or woman was central to this study, this identification was not a single generalized experience: "Woman itself is a contested and fractured terrain . . . the experience of 'woman' is always constituted by subjects with vastly different interests" (Nash, 2008, p. 3). Each of our identities, including our gender identities, was nuanced (Nash, 2008) by our experiences. Feminism served as a strong theoretical framework throughout this project, influencing the questions we asked, the ways we made meaning, and our commitment to community engagement and activism. Feminism was a frequent theme during our team meetings. To better situate our experiences with a broader feminist dialogue, I offered the students some reading on feminist theory and scholarship. This often led to charged conversation about gender, justice, and power. Figure 1 offers a working definition and five assumptions we used to guide how feminism was operationalized in our work. These assumptions were directly informed by our dialogues and readings.

As a research team, we believed that personal stories were imperative and powerful tools both for making meaning and making a difference. We explored, interrogated, and shared the experiences we had interacting in social spaces, including school, the local community, sports, extracurricular activities, and religious institutions. As young women, the students in our research groups expressed concerns during the transition period from high school to college that were directly related to gender (Snyder, 2008), including identity (Shields, 2004), discrimination (Collins, 2000), safety (hooks, 2000), and stereotyping (Adichie, 2014). These concerns were heightened by the context of preparing to live on their own at campuses away from their families. Gendered and sexual violence (Adichie, 2014; Collins, 2000; hooks, 2000) on potential college campuses was a serious factor that the students, and their parents, considered as they made their college decisions.

The students participated in activities that were still dominated by young men, including sports, science, math, and technology. The student researchers continued to pursue these interests in their collegiate studies. In high school, the heteronormativity of prom was another instance when gender and sexual identity were foregrounded. The cultural hegemonic trope of a young woman and young man attending prom as potential romantic part-

---

Feminism: a movement to expand equity, legitimize women's lived experiences, and end sexism and oppression.

> We need a **change agenda** focused on **equity**.
> The current social order marginalizes **women's lived experiences**.
> Aggressions against women and girls are both **overt and covert**.
> Gender is a **social construct**.
> **Personal stories matter** in political movements.

FIGURE 1. Guiding assumptions, feminism.

---

ners was a mismatch for many of the students on our research teams, who chose either not to attend prom, to attend with a platonic friend, or to go with a group of young women friends. In short, what the student researchers believed about being young women was often at odds with mainstream messaging they received about gender. Sometimes this mismatch was a source of conflict, while other times it was a source of pride.

Our project brings to light the rich, complex—and messy—stories of the student researchers. This work is in the spirit of Belenky et al.'s (1997) foundational text, *Women's Ways of Knowing*. Within this study, Belenky et al. identified a concept called "constructed knowledge," where women made

> effort[s] to reclaim the self by attempting to integrate knowledge they felt intuitively was personally important with knowledge they had learned from others. They told of weaving together the strands of rational and emotive thought and integrating objective and subjective knowing. (p. 134)

During our research, we paid particular attention to the unique multiple identities and lived experiences we all brought to this project. Our research team explored the ways that personal stories both countered and mapped against cultural and political trends. Inherent in this project was an unmasking (through art, activism, and radio storytelling) of new narratives about being a high-achieving young woman.

Youth Participatory Action Research

Youth participatory action research (YPAR) is a qualitative methodology that provides an alternative and empowering forum for conducting research with student communities (Taylor et al., 2006). YPAR projects address practical problems or issues in student communities (Heron & Reason, 2001). In our case, we addressed the affective crisis for gifted and high-achieving young women. Although the particulars of each YPAR project are unique, there are a number of underlying tenets that inform YPAR work, including investigating a problem or issue, engaging individual and community reflection, taking action that benefits the people involved in the research project as well as their communities, and building cooperative alliances between researchers and "participants" (McIntyre, 2008). The participant-to-researcher relationship is intentionally disrupted in participatory projects, so that instead of viewing students as participants, facilitators of YPAR projects engage in coresearch with student researchers (Taylor et al., 2006). For a more detailed overview of YPAR, please see the Methodology Appendix.

Throughout our projects, the student researchers and I made sense of our experiences, data, and the ways we wanted to share our findings together. When I introduced this project to the students, the first question they asked me was, "What are we were looking for?" They wanted specifics and preferably an answer they could verify and calculate. Several students asked me how we could graph our findings. Most of the students had only participated in research projects through experiments in their science classes. As a team of high-achieving students, they approached this project with pointed intentionality. Each of us, in our own ways, wanted to proverbially solve for x. Throughout our work, we engaged in a collective unlearning about this positivist and deductive approach to research. The students on the research teams were accustomed to finding the "right" answer. One of the lessons we learned through this project was the importance of many "right" answers. Part II explores these findings in greater detail.

ELAINE'S JOURNAL
Senior in High School

February 14, 2015

It's been about 3 months since the last time I wrote and man so much has happened. I got into the University of W. and I'm still waiting on M. and B. I doubt I'll get in, but at least I have W. I just can't stay here anymore. I don't have anything against [hometown University], but I feel like being gay would be easier living somewhere else. I told mom and dad that I'm gay. They thought I was going through a phase and my mom wanted me to go see a psychiatrist but I said NO. I was so hurt that they didn't think I was old enough or smart enough to know. They explained that "later" *if* I'm gay, they would love me no matter what and nothing would change, which is better than what some kids have to go through so Imma [I am going to] take it. It definitely was awkward for a while after that, but things blew over and are pretty normal now.

I made the state band on alto (3rd) and bari [baritone saxophone] (2nd) and I made callbacks for jazz on guitar, which was sweet. I definitely wasn't expecting to make bari because I didn't even practice the music. As for Calculus III, I got a 95% on the final, keeping my A in the class and my 4.0, which was a relief. I remember walking out really upset because I didn't finish. I remember my dad took me out to get frozen yogurt though, which made me feel a little better. At that point I just got out of knee surgery for my meniscus so I was worried about what I was eating since I couldn't work out. My knee is feeling a lot better now. I'm sure future me remembers making a fool of myself the day after surgery when I went to band rehearsal on pain meds. That's all I'm gunna say about that . . .

Senior year so far has been great.

PART II

Cultivating Courage, Connection, and Self-Care in Schools

Title

Animatronic

Artist

Joanna (2014), senior in high school

Artist Notes

This piece reflects the endless hours of practice athletes put into their sports. Sometimes we practice to the point that our actions flow with robotic precision and the original passion is lost to rote repetition. By senior year, it's easy for students to have burnt out from a high school career's worth of practice, and college applications only add to the disenchantment. We trained until our performances are an engineered perfection and as we fill out application forms our sports are reduced into a set of numbers and awards.

Our research pointed to three broad, related themes: courage, connection, and self-care. Part II analyzes each of these themes respectively. These were neither separate nor isolated; rather, they worked in concert and conversation with each other. For example, we found that courage was reciprocally—although not necessarily linearly—related to the ways we understood and experienced connection and self-care. In fact, if we were interested in one theme, it usually helped us to evaluate how much attention we were giving to the other two themes. For example, if we wanted to be more courageous, we found that nurturing our connections and prioritizing self-care often led to the conditions we needed to practice more courage. These three themes are cornerstones for the Wholehearted Teaching framework described in Part III.

MINDY
An Abridged Case Study

Mindy joined Barnwood as a junior and quickly made a home in the gifted room. She wrote detailed AP tutorials on the whiteboard in our classroom. Students would review her tutorials over lunch in preparation for labs or exams. Mindy received national recognition for her extraordinarily high standardized test scores. Although intensely bright, she often struggled to turn in her work. It was not uncommon for her homework to be months late. More than once, teachers came to me concerned that Mindy would fail their classes. With a lot of work, tears, and too little sleep, she always managed to get all of her work in and finish her courses with strong grades.

One afternoon, a few months after Mindy joined Barnwood, I looked across my classroom and saw her sobbing uncontrollably. It was lunchtime, and the room was very crowded. Most students were absorbed in frantic studying, lunchtime conversations, or playing board games; they didn't notice her. I raced over to Mindy. She didn't respond when I bent down to talk to her. It seemed like she was in another world. I looked to her friends nearby.

One of them said, "It's okay. I know what to do. We've done this before."

The friend took Mindy's glasses; Mindy blinked and rubbed her eyes. Her friend put her arm around Mindy's shoulder and gently rubbed her long black hair. After several minutes, she calmed down. The next day everything appeared normal again, and Mindy assured me things were fine.

Things were not fine.

Over the 2 years Mindy studied at Barnwood, she and I worked closely together. A talented therapist from our school counseling team partnered with me to support Mindy. Over the next several months, we worked with Mindy on a self-care practice that included walking, deep breathing, and regular check-ins.

After months of focusing on self-care and connection, Mindy opened up to me about an unhealthy situation at home. It was an hour or so after lunch. We were the only two people in the gifted room. I had just made her a cup of tea.

"I have something to tell you," she said.

It took tremendous courage for her to share her story. These circumstances and this story were not new; in fact, Mindy had been struggling for years. However, it took the right conditions for her to feel safe enough to share this difficult situation and to ask for help. Being able to ask for help is a powerful action that cuts across courage, connection, and self-care. We need to normalize asking for help in schools. And when we hear a call for help, we need to support teachers in responding with empathy and compassion.

CHAPTER 3

Courage

Title

Selfie

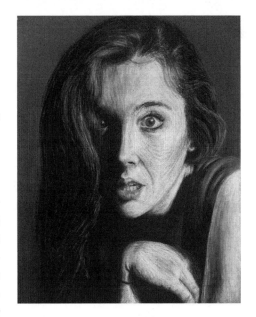

Artist

Megan Kelly (2014), senior in high school

Artist Notes

This self-portrait is a comment on society's obsession with the "selfie" and how we have become a social media-based culture. There is this pressure to fit in and be beautiful. It can start to overpower you. For me, it has made me judge myself more. This drawing is supposed to break those boundaries of what is beautiful with the funny expression as well as the extreme use of white. The drawing is supposed to show that there are many "colors" in everyone but they can be overpowered and drained out by our surroundings.

Courage takes many forms: a comment, a piece of art, a story, an apology, a choice to participate, a choice to not participate, a call for help. In this chapter, I discuss how we named and experienced courage within broader systems of school and society. I close this chapter with an important pattern we noticed: that courage can lead to a ripple effect in communities.

Naming Courage

We all came to this research with preconceived (and ultimately incomplete) ideas about vulnerability. We associated vulnerability with feeling less than or weaker. When she joined our research team, I asked Elaine, a varsity athlete and valedictorian, what she thought of vulnerability. She considered and then told me,

> Well, I hate wearing swimsuits. I feel like people will judge me, so I avoid water at all costs during the summer. I've felt this way since I was like 5, and I think I know where it stemmed from. When I was younger, [my brother] was always super skinny. He teased me for being fat, which made me believe I was fat all the way up till today. . . . Admitting that is something that makes me feel vulnerable. It is embarrassing, and I don't like to talk about it too often. When I get invited to swim I always say I haven't swam since, like, the fourth grade, which is true. Some of my friends do see through it and say I don't need to be insecure, which I hate hearing because it sounds weak to me.

Instead of feeling "insecure" and "weak," we found that sharing our vulnerable stories often made us feel stronger and more connected. This directly contradicted what we thought we knew about vulnerability. In fact, we were frequently surprised by how strength and vulnerability worked together. The students tested this relationship in our research luncheons and their other peer groups, and repeatedly found that vulnerable story sharing, although difficult, felt personally empowering and led to stronger relationships. Our team was excited about this relationship between vulnerability and strength. It quickly led to an engaged exploration in my classroom. The students asked: Why—and under what conditions—did vulnerability make us feel stronger as opposed to weaker? They got to work tackling this question as if it were a complex logic problem.

They drew diagrams to illustrate different relationships between strength and vulnerability. They asked their peers for their opinions on how to connect vulnerability with strength, and guardedness with limitation. At one point, a small group of students was using calculus to explain a four-dimensional model that related strength, vulnerability, guardedness, and limitations. The energy in my classroom was palpable. Two students jotted complicated notes on the back of an envelope they found on my desk.

Patiently, they told me that a four-dimensional model made the most sense because it could also include motion: "Look, if we want to account for all the possibilities of how strength and vulnerability could be related, we need to put this model in motion."

A student started diagramming how to add guardedness and limitations into this new model. A few minutes later, she crossed off the figure on the envelope. She called over to another advanced math student. It felt as though we were onto something big. And we were. However, like any breakthrough, it took work.

When we reached a standstill, I encouraged the students to use their reflective journals to share stories about times when they felt vulnerable or guarded, strong or limited. I suggested that if we better understood how these concepts worked in our own lives, we might better understand the connection between strength and vulnerability. The next day, the student researchers reflected on their experiences with courage.

STUDENT RESEARCHERS' NOTES ON COURAGE

It takes courage to be vulnerable enough to empathize with others. One must be open and transparent because that is the only way . . . [to] develop meaningful relationships with others. Being honest and truthful is the only way to build trust. But, we will be the first to admit that it is difficult at times to be honest. Certainly, telling others your secrets and sensitive information is hard, but we think the real challenge is being frank and honest with yourself. . . . The first step then, is to tell ourselves the truth, and that takes strength and vulnerability because sometimes the truth is not what you want to hear. Overall, though, we think that vulnerability is the basis of empathy and that the outcome of being vulnerable and raw is that others will connect with you. . . . Oftentimes, people are very guarded, and it is hard to tell if you actually mean something to them and if they are being truthful with you. Thus, we believe that everyone should practice being vulnerable. If we all did that, the world would be a much more understanding place.

This reflection was the first time the student researchers named courage as essential to practicing vulnerability. They also linked it directly to connection and empathy. We used this reflection as a springboard to defining courage. After much deliberation, we defined courage as the emotional fortitude linking strength to vulnerability. Naming courage gave us a common language to explore and navigate countless situations in school and life.

Contrast Elaine's reflection (see p. 48) about feeling insecure as a weakness (which was written before we named courage) with the following quote from Faith (which was written after we had named courage). Faith, a high school valedictorian, practiced strong vulnerability through openly sharing her struggles with depression, anxiety, and eating disorders:

> I'm definitely vulnerable, but I feel like the fact that I'm willing to share my vulnerabilities and I don't let them rule . . . my life (or at least I'm working toward that) or cause me to live in fear makes me strong. I think that we're expected to be so close-lipped about insecurities and pretend like everything's fine but that's not a good idea. Talking about our vulnerabilities openly promotes understanding and education and also just helps in general.

Faith was able to identify with strength, not in spite of her vulnerabilities, but because of her willingness to share them. Her assertion that "talking about our vulnerabilities openly . . . helps" became a central belief that guided our research and activism through the tumultuous landscape of power, privilege, and challenge.

Courage Is Contextualized by Power

Power and privilege interact with courage in important ways. The student researchers were committed to initiating new conversations about gender, race, culture, sexual orientation, and class. Given their own personal identities (e.g., woman, Chinese, gay, Lutheran) and experiences, these topics mattered to the students individually; however, identity is also contextualized by broader systems of advantage and disadvantage.

For example, several of the student researchers spoke of hesitating before identifying as a feminist on college applications. As a senior in high school, Melissa said,

> I was writing on the women's empowerment group about being a feminist and I thought, "Do I really want to draw attention to this?" I had that doubt. And then I was like, "Wait, definitely!" But you're trained to think that someone somewhere will take that negatively.

The student researchers shared that although they sometimes hesitated when identifying with a minority group, they felt the risk was usually worth "being true" to their identity and beliefs. Being a part of a minority group was context-specific and could include race and ethnicity, as well as being a feminist, a woman in STEM, a Christian, or a woman athlete.

Elaine said she often experienced lower expectations as an athlete because of both her Asian American identity and her identity as young woman. She wrote on this topic in one of her college essays.

EXCERPT FROM ELAINE'S SCHOLARSHIP ESSAY
Senior in High School

May 2015

As an Asian American girl enrolled in multiple AP courses and deeply involved in my school's band program, I should have come to expect the judgment of my new peers as I entered the first day of practice to throw the shot put and discus for Barnwood's track and field team, events that require intense speed and power. Standing next to the other girls, I could almost feel myself practically shrinking next to their built frames and looming heights, and I could tell by the way the coach critically looked me up and down that there was no doubt in either of our minds as to who had the upper hand. . . . During partner drills, while everyone else paired up quickly, I was always everyone's last choice. . . . My stereotype defined who they thought me to be as a meek Asian girl, but that wasn't who I was.

. . . I enrolled in Advanced Strength Training, a class full of hefty football players and strong female basketball players. There I felt the same judgment. . . . Without even giving me a chance to lift, they already decided I didn't have what it took to make gains. . . . Once during a workout, I fell doing a hang clean, one of the more advanced Olympic lifts. Snickers filled the room. . . . Sometimes I would go to my designated rack, and my straps would be gone. Sometimes other athletes would find it amusing to cover my view of the mirror during Romanian deadlifts. It was difficult to keep going when I knew my peers were only expecting me to fail, and there were times when I didn't want to have anything to do with athletics for this reason.

The judgment and bullying Elaine experienced in athletics was gendered and raced ("as an Asian American girl"). It is also important to note that the adults in the system failed to intervene in this bullying and judgment. Even worse, Elaine perceived that her coach initially shared in the student stereotypes. Elaine told us that although it was very difficult, she used this unequal treatment as motivation to work hard and "prove them wrong." During the course of my research, Elaine was named "All State" in shot put and went on to win a gold medal at our state games in the Olympic lifting category.

These raced and gendered conversations and experiences within systems of power and privilege were emotionally charged. When the student researchers chose to practice courage and speak back to systems of injustice, they often experienced intense emotions. Students need safe spaces to explore and process difficult and intense emotions and situations.

The Importance of Safe Space in Schools

A safe space is a welcoming, supportive space that is physically and emotionally safe (Kosciw, Greytak, Giga, Villenas, & Danischewski, 2016). The term *safe space* was originally used as part of an effort to create inclusive spaces for LGBTQ youth. The research on LGBTQ students and mental health is alarming. For LGBTQ youth ages 10–24, suicide is one of the leading causes of death; these youth are 4 times more likely to attempt suicide and 6 times more likely to experience symptoms of depression than the general population (National Alliance on Mental Illness [NAMI], 2018). According to Kosciw et al. (2016),

> We know that school is not always a safe place for LGBT students. Most LGBT students frequently hear anti-LGBT language and experience harassment related to their sexual orientation and gender expression, and the majority of LGBT students feel unsafe at school and are likely to skip class or even full days of school to avoid the anti-LGBT name-calling, bullying and harassment they face on a daily basis. But educators can make a big difference. (p. 2)

Indeed, research supports that schools are critical spaces where students either experience inclusion and affirmation or exclusion and rejection. The former obviously has positive impacts of development and well-being, and the latter can be detrimental. Wholehearted teachers create safe spaces for all students to grow and learn.

This term *safe space* has now been expanded to broader inclusive practices in schools. For example, school equity teams and social justice educators often reference creating safe spaces for students, making sure marginalized populations (e.g., racial minorities, students with disabilities, and homeless youth) have safe spaces to be included among their peers and to share their stories and experiences without risk of bullying. Our research objectives included opening up dialogues about difference, forging new friendships, and engaging in courageous story sharing. These acts are only possible in spaces where students feel safe to fully explore their feelings and be themselves.

When we set personal goals in our empowerment group, Elaine shared that she wanted to tell her best friend that she was gay. During our project she had several coming out experiences: to her parents, to me, to college admissions committees, and to our research team. However, she was most nervous about coming out to her best friend. Currently, there is little research on LGBTQ youth who have also been identified as gifted (Cohn, 2002). Cohn wrote, "the sense of vulnerability among these youths may be most affected by those mainstream adults in their lives who bear silent witness to acts of hate and intolerance around them" (p. 146). The risks associated with Elaine coming out were based on patterns of homophobia and heterosexism that we had seen in our schools and communities. Her personal identity was politically charged not because of who she is attracted to, but because of a larger system of hegemonic heteronormativity that marginalizes sexual orientations that fall outside of the dominant group. This is why it would have been a non-story if one of the other student researchers came out as being straight. The risks of telling counterhegemonic stories are real and can be difficult to navigate. Elaine told me that although her coming-out experiences had been "mostly okay," she had experienced bullying, including being punched and called a derogatory name in reference to her sexual orientation. It was clear that the memory was still painful and raw as she told me pieces of the story.

Elaine set a deadline to come out to her best friend 2 weeks before she left for college. She talked to me at length about this. One day we met at a park for a walking dialogue. When I checked my pedometer, we had walked more than 5 miles. Elaine was deeply invested in her relationship with her best friend, which made the risks higher. Elaine worried that her friend would think less of her and ultimately reject her. Her best friend was another young woman on the track and field team. Their relationship began as teammates and lifting partners; however, over the track season it grew into a deeper friendship. At our final team celebration, Elaine shared this coming-out poem she had written for her friend.

ELAINE'S POEM TO HER BEST FRIEND

August 2015

Dear B.,
I have something I've been wanting to tell you.
I've been keeping it to myself . . .
When you claim that I am "grumpy,"
you're so good at making me smile.
And for that reason,
I wanna keep you around for a while.
But if you're gunna be in my life any longer,
I need to tell you something about me
that will hopefully only make our friendship stronger.
 . . . Usually, I wouldn't say a thing,
But I think you deserve to know.
How can I call you a close friend,
if I can't share this with you, and just keep it hidden down below.
 . . . I don't know how I waited
this long to this day.
But I've been wanting so badly to tell you
that I, Elaine Pho, am gay.
 . . . You told me, I remember
that you're supposed to love thy neighbor.
So I hope that means we can stay the same,
I hope we can stay the way we were.
But I know you also grew up believing
That marriage should be between those of the opposite sex.
So I understand if you never want to see me again,
or converse over text.
 . . . Really, your love and support
Is all I need.
I don't think this makes me a bad person,
I've never committed any terrible deeds.
 . . . I don't mean to do this to you,
And put you on the spot.
I really care about you, B.

I care about you a lot.
 . . . And dear B.,
There is one last thing I need to tell you before I go.
I really didn't choose this life.
If someone asked me to be gay, I would have said no.
But I have accepted myself for who I am,
And I hope you can do the same.
We have quite the history together,
Too many great memories to just throw away.
 . . . Until then,
I wish you the best of luck in everything you pursue.
Imma miss you hellas [I'm going to miss you a hell of a lot].
Yours truly, Pho

Elaine drew on our research team dialogues about the interrelated nature of connection, courage, and self-care as she authored and ultimately shared this poem with her best friend. She decided that if she and her friend were to continue to have a deep connection, then their friendship needed honesty and disclosure. This was congruent with our research team conversations that being "true to yourself" is both an act of courage and self-care.

Elaine knew that she and her best friend came from different political, religious, and cultural backgrounds. She knew that these various social identities contributed to differing worldviews, and she worried about how her friend would negotiate her religious identity and their friendship. Throughout her poem, Elaine used many of the tools we discussed and practiced in our project. She employed courage, vulnerability, storytelling, and creative writing to both make peace with herself—"I have accepted myself for who I am"—and to open up to her best friend. For Elaine, being honest and open about who she was to the people she cared about was a practice in self-care. Shortly after she shared the poem at our team celebration, Elaine found the courage to read it to her friend. Afterward she sent me the following text:

> **Elaine:** I saw B. tonight and told her before I went home. It went really well! I read her the poem and she said she didn't care at all and that nothing changes! We ended up talking for another hour and half maybe. What a great night!

Kathryn: I am SO glad.
Elaine: Thanks! I'm super hyped.

I was truly relieved. Elaine told me that through our research she learned how much relationships matter. She said she was grateful to now have more honest relationships with the people she loved, including her parents and close friends. I hope Elaine also learned that her words have power, and that her story is important. There are enough pressures and struggles during the vibrant and tumultuous high school and college years—being accepted for who you are and affirmed as a valued member of your school community should never be one of them. Wholehearted Teaching advances safe space culture at school so that when students share their lived experiences it is not an act of courage, but rather an act of connection. We have a long way to go to achieve this inclusive reality.

Courage Is Emotionally Charged

Being courageous is an emotional experience. Emotions and feelings were central to our discussions and work. In particular, we identified a cyclical relationship between strong emotions and vulnerability. Being vulnerable caused strong emotions, and having strong emotions caused us to feel vulnerable, which, in turn contributed to more strong emotions. This cycle could be both positive and negative. Melissa described a panic attack she experienced during her senior year of high school.

MELISSA'S JOURNAL
Senior in High School

May 15, 2015

I started to have a full-blown panic attack in the back seat. And it lasted like 10 minutes and I couldn't breathe and it was horrible. But it was worse because it almost felt like I was proving the point. I don't know why I reacted so badly. Most of the time when people upset me I don't let them know unless I'm reacting jokingly angry or something. No one has ever seen me have a panic attack, because I don't get them as often as I do

the unnoticeable kind. . . . And my friends have never just [seen me] completely out of control in a blind panic when I feel like I'm about to die. I
don't like feeling weak and I don't like making other people feel bad. . . . I
just want for all my feelings to go away sometimes. I feel trapped by them
and I hate feeling sad or guilty or just over-emotional. But I can't help it
and I can't control them so I try to minimize their impact on other people
and I've been doing a terrible job and yeah.

Melissa's journal speaks to several of the layers of the masked affective
crisis. She felt compelled to hide her emotions ("Most of the time when
people upset me, I don't let them know it"), particularly her strongest and
most difficult emotions. She associated being emotional with being weak.
She felt guilty about having such strong emotions and shame about the ways
they interfered with her friendships and relationships. However, holding
in, hiding, and masking these kinds of emotions led to real consequences,
including physical panic attacks. Many of the young women who participated in this research project spoke of having similar panic attacks during
high school and college.

In our empowerment group, we discussed how emotions are gendered.
Being emotional is often associated with femininity, and because of hegemonic masculinity, the connotation is often that being emotional means
being weaker or less capable. Our research around courage contradicted
this assumption; therefore, we wanted to reframe and normalize experiencing the full range of emotions. Philosophically, we were in unanimous con-
sensus about this; practically, however, we found that resocializing ourselves
was more challenging than we had anticipated. Owning our emotions felt
uncomfortable and risky (we wondered how we would be judged). However,
like our experience with other courageous acts, including personal story
sharing and asking for help, we found that usually we felt stronger and more
connected when we chose honesty and sharing instead of masking and
guarding.

This didn't mean we were always (or even often) comfortable with vulnerability. By nature, being vulnerable was usually uncomfortable. One
afternoon Elaine and I were talking in the quiet annex outside of the gifted
room, and she started crying. Afterward, she apologized. I asked what she
was apologizing for, and she said, "For crying in front of you. I told you I
would never do that." Although I didn't remember her original promise to

not cry in front of me, I was struck by the fact that it was still so difficult to express intense emotions.

ELAINE'S JOURNAL
Senior in High School

May 12, 2015

I hate crying . . . because society makes it so that females are the emotionally weak and unstable ones because they tend to shed more tears than guys and because of that, men are not just viewed as "physically stronger" but "emotionally stronger/stable." I find that VERY insulting, so I guess my hate for crying stems from trying to prove the stigma wrong that I'm not a cry baby female who is unstable and can't handle my emotions because I have hormones and deal with mother nature every month. Forreal [sic]. Why can't guys get over themselves and cry? Who cares if their eyes produce salty water?

Emotionally, I'd like to think I'm always strong. I don't like tears. Although, as much as I hate to admit it, Elaine Pho can produce water from her eyes depending on the circumstances. I always say it's okay for people to cry, and I truly believe it. If one of my friends started crying over the smallest thing, I would still give them a hug and tell them everything will be alright. . . . Although I think it is okay for people to cry, I don't think it is okay for me to cry. I hate doing it, and it embarrasses me when I get to the point where I have to fight back tears. That track meet this past Friday was one of them. I don't even like to cry in front of my own mom. Having to hold them back in front of my coach was awful. I feel weak when I do cry, and I also feel like people always expect me to be the strong one who keeps my head up when all cray [the craziness] breaks loose.

Elaine and I discussed this particular journal at some length. We talked about wanting to normalize emotions for many groups, including young men, athletes, and high-achieving women. Although Elaine wanted to help normalize strong emotions and crying for others, she was not comfortable crying in front of others. Many of the young women on our research teams held themselves to a similar emotional double standard (i.e., "It is okay for you to cry, but not for me").

Sometimes, such as in the reflection Melissa shared about her panic attack, the students told me that they felt their emotions were "too powerful." There were times when they spoke about being frustrated by their intense emotions. For example, just before high school commencement in 2015, Leslie reflected back on her senior year and shared,

> I think my emotional volatility has had a negative effect on many of my relationships this year with my family and friends. I regret that I have been all over the place this year. But, I think that this year has been particularly stressful on me so I have been even more emotionally weak than normal.

I encouraged the student researchers (and myself) to challenge the hegemonic belief that being strong emotionally also means being guarded. The following is an excerpt from a conversation with Elaine on this topic.

> **Kathryn:** "I wonder if there is strength in being able to cry in front of others, to be okay and say, hey, this is a strong feeling I am having right now."
> **Elaine:** "I guess there's strength in being able to cry in front of others. I personally don't view others as weak when they cry because I completely get it. When you're sad, you're sad, and it's nice to see that some people don't care what others think when they cry. I only view myself as weak when I cry because I feel like people expect me to be strong."

I suggested that it took courage to share difficult or intense emotions, particularly in a society where high-achieving young women—and men—feel they need to hide their emotions. During this project, we tried to approach our intense emotions with strength and courage. This meant, allowing ourselves to feel, own, and name our emotions. Approaching feelings in this openhearted way was another important act of courage we identified. This was deeply personal work.

During the course of our research, almost all of us shed tears. Many of us, including me, were surprised at the tears that fell. The more we paid attention to the outcomes of our strong emotions, the more our emotions surprised us with their power. As we shared our stories, particularly our most vulnerable stories, we were often caught off guard by the powerful emotions these stories elicited.

I started listening to my own inner dialogue when I found myself crying. I noticed that my first response (like the students') was to try to stop the tears immediately. After my conversations with the students in our empowerment groups, I changed my approach. Instead, I tried naming and affirming the emotion I was having. In this way, during our research project, I allowed myself to mourn my aunt's passing more completely. In addition to exploring how we experienced intense emotions, we also paid attention to when we experienced these emotions. Antecedents for panic attacks included high-stakes assessments and applications, school stressors, and the particularity of being gifted/perfectionist/high-achieving. Many of the students on our research teams experienced these panic attacks, but most had not talked to their peers about them before joining our group and were surprised to learn that they weren't "the only one" having these intense emotions.

Precipice and the Possibility for Courage

We often referenced "the precipice" as a metaphor for the emotional state before a major life event (e.g., leaving for college). As a new gifted education teacher, I felt uncomfortable with the fear and exhilaration of the precipice. I wanted to reconstruct this experience to something safer and more positive, like a springboard. When I first started teaching in gifted education I wanted to lessen struggle and fear. I thought compassionate teaching meant easing my students' hardships. Looking back, this feels naive.

Through our research, I found that often the challenges our students face are not too big; instead, our school systems fail to equip them with the skill set of courage, self-care, strength, vulnerability, compassion, and connection to face these challenges. The metaphor of the precipice remained relevant to our transition experiences and to our lessons on courage. This metaphor was solidified during our student art showcase, "Perspectives on the Precipice." Our association with being on a precipice evolved over time. The more we learned about courage and crisis, the more we saw both how challenge is inevitable and how it can be beneficial. Sure, a precipice is scary; sometimes though, it is also exciting. Courage, like other skills, only becomes salient when it is used. We began to explore precipices in our lives, beginning with an immediate one—high school graduation. The day after her high school commencement ceremony, Faith shared the following journal with me.

FAITH'S JOURNAL
Valedictorian, Recent High School Graduate

May 23, 2015

A precipice makes me picture that you are at the top of a mountain that you've climbed and you're looking out over the whole world, and you see so many different things and you're unsure of what to do with it all. Previously your view has been obscured or you haven't been able to picture what it would be like once you got to the top because you were so focused on the journey there. But now you're at the top and if you want to take a chance in any one of those things, you'd have to jump off the precipice, which takes a LOT of courage. But at the same time, jumping off is the only way to move forward, because you cannot stand at the precipice forever, nor should you. I feel like that really describes our high school to college transition.

The precipice is always accompanied by intense emotions. Over time, we learned to associate the precipice with an opportunity to practice courage. As Faith said, "If you want to take a chance in any one of those things, you'd have to jump off the precipice, which takes a LOT of courage." The transition from high school to college was the first precipice we discussed, because it was so central to our study. We also explored the sense of relief students felt after being on the other side of a precipice.

As a musical theater student, Molly underwent rigorous singing and dancing auditions as part of her college applications. Once she was accepted into a college program, she shared that she felt as though a huge weight had been lifted and she could finally be her "true self." Just before her high school graduation in 2014, Molly told me:

> Because I know where I am going to college, the whole idea of judgment has kind of left! I am going to a school to pursue what I love. That has given me so much confidence. I

find myself not worrying as much about what I look or act like either, partially because I'm think[ing] to myself "who cares? I may never see some of these people again!" So in a sense I am really being myself for the first time in high school and I like it! I really hope I am able to continue this next year.

Similarly, a few days after her high school graduation in 2014, Mira told me,

I used to have a lot of fears about how people would perceive or judge me. I felt like I had to get into an Ivy League school or have a perfect GPA in order to prove myself not only to others, but to myself. I truly felt that my desire for academic perfection defined me. But I lost my 4.0.

Mira graduated with a 3.99. I knew it wouldn't do any good to comment that a 3.99 is academic perfection. She continued:

I didn't get accepted to any Ivies. And yet, I feel beautiful. I really did try my best. I could be bitter that 9 out of the 12 colleges I applied to apparently didn't care for me, but . . . isn't it kind of their loss? I'm actually going to get my long wavy hair cut very short in a few days. Like, boy-short. I hope that if you look over and catch a glimpse at me as you're reading this, you see a girl with short hair. Because I'm finally free, and it feels awesome.

A couple of weeks later, Mira cut her hair.

By adopting a common language around transition, we started to recognize precipice experiences in our lives beyond just high school graduation. These included any major transition where courage was required to navigate uncertain emotional or physical terrain. With this operational definition in place, precipice experiences, and therefore opportunities to practice courage, were suddenly everywhere. These included making a college decision, moving away, having a surgery, and mourning a loved one.

During our research, I reflected on my own life and considered my own graduations. I paused, remembering more personal precipices: my marriage, the adoption of our son, the death of two of my grandparents, the birth of my daughter. I thought of the imposter phenomenon I had experi-

63

enced at each new job I had taken, including the position I accepted at the close of this project as the Director of Academic Affairs for a K–12 school system. I realized that at each of the precipices, I, too, had used courage, connection, and self-care to navigate my way.

On my first day in my new position, Melissa texted me, "I AM SO EXCITED FOR YOU! You are the one who's taught me the most about making transitions through life so it seems fitting that we are going through one at the same time." Melissa's suggestion that I was a precipice mentor gave me the confidence to approach my first day in my new position with courage.

Although we do not always get to choose our precipices or their outcomes, we can choose our outlooks and actions. The precipices encountered during our research were marked by both positive and negative life changes (e.g., getting accepted to college, a parent losing a job, reporting an abusive relationship, receiving a new medical diagnosis, choosing a major, etc.). I am not suggesting that individual acts of courage, even coupled with connection and self-care, are all it takes to "get through" the varied precipices our students encounter. Some of the crises the student researchers shared were products of broader systems of inequality, including sexism, racism, classism, and heterosexism. There were several times during my teaching career when violence, aggression, or bullying necessitated that I work with outside agencies, including law enforcement, to ensure the safety of one of the high-achieving young women in my program. To suggest that courage, connection, and self-care would have been sufficient interventions is short-sighted. However, even in extreme cases, we found that these themes were critical components to the healing and growing process.

The Ripple Effect of Practicing Courage

The student researchers discovered that an act of courage often led to other acts of courage. One afternoon during our research, Leslie was working in the gifted resource room. While she was studying, a group of high school students began talking about weight. A young man shared that he was "disgusted by overweight people." Before I could intervene, a few other young women spoke up, asking him pointed questions about health and gender. Although he didn't rescind his remarks or apologize, he struggled to defend his position. A few minutes later, the bell rang and the group scattered. Leslie asked the young man to come over and talk to her. She had not yet participated in the conversation.

The young man walked over to her. I wondered what she was going to say and was struck by her courage when she asked, "Do I disgust you?"

He floundered and choked out, "Of course not."

Leslie said, "Well, wasn't that your argument?"

At that moment, several of Leslie's friends came running into the gifted room. Oblivious to what had just happened, they jumped in with some exciting social news. Leslie flashed them a giant smile, enveloping them in a hug. The young man quietly left the room.

When he arrived to school early the next morning, I sat down with him to process what had happened. I was ready with a carefully prepared "teaching conversation." However, before I had a chance, he told me,

> I made a mistake yesterday. That was a really dumb thing I said. I could see that it was stupid pretty quickly, but I didn't know how to back down. Then, when Leslie asked if I was disgusted by her, I realized just how big I'd messed up. Last night I called her and everyone else who was in the room and apologized. I promise I'll be more careful about the things I say.

By using the courage to make an issue personal, Leslie helped her classmate see a new perspective. Although Leslie's courageous approach had inspired me, I was even more moved by the impact it had on the young man. Leslie taught her classmate to think more deeply about the implications of his words. She also inspired him to engage in another courageous act—apologizing. Later that day I talked to Leslie about what happened. I did not have a good teaching conversation ready for that exchange. In fact, it was obvious to me that she had been the better teacher in that particular moment. She told me that it had taken courage to make the conversation personal, but that she also knew doing so might "wake him up" to what he was saying.

Throughout our project we learned that courage often requires taking the difficult but "right" path. Taking this path always requires strength (usually emotional strength). We talked about risk, how we often felt vulnerable in sharing difficult truths (e.g., struggling with mental health, feeling ashamed about our cultures, and being bullied). However, there were great rewards (e.g., stronger connections and inspiring courage in others) for taking these risks. As we practiced courage, we became more courageous, and in turn we looked for more opportunities to show emotional fortitude around the issues we cared about.

Toward the end of our project, a student from Leslie's new college reached out to her over social media. As they talked, Leslie told him about our research project, including the lessons we had learned on vulnerability, achievement, hope, and self-doubt. She was excited to tell me this about their exchange.

LESLIE'S JOURNAL
Ivy League Student

July 8, 2015

I firmly believe that the assumption that successful people always have their lives together is really holding us back and holding affective education back. Why should more money be put into gifted education, [if] they are already smart and successful? That's what a lot of people think. They are wrong. We shared a lot of personal information and we were both very vulnerable. Through that discourse, we discovered that we had a lot of the same fears about [Ivy League school].

. . . And then he asked me "so what gives you hope?" That question blindsided me. At first, I didn't know what to say. Because just a few weeks ago, I would have said that there wasn't a lot of hope. Just a few weeks ago, I would have said that I think I am going to fail out of [Ivy League school]—don't ask me. But that wasn't what I wanted to say. So something changed. Something inside of me has changed so that I am not so pessimistic and negative. Don't get me wrong, I still have self-doubts, but I realized tonight that I am getting better. And that made me happy.

Leslie's observations and reflections that her work on courage, connection, and self-care resulted in a happier and more hopeful self-concept are significant. In her text, Leslie also speaks to the persistence of self-doubt among high-achieving students, and the misconception that gifted students do not need affective education.

The student researchers used storytelling, vulnerability, and strength to practice courage and make a difference regarding issues that were important to their personal experiences and their social-emotional needs. They worked to make a difference for others but often found that this work influenced them on a personal level. They learned they were more courageous than they had thought. The student researchers opened up to each other, their families, their peers, the community, and even to strangers. In doing so, they found that emotional strength rests, not in masking difficult feelings, but in embracing them, in leaning into the breeze on the precipice, and saying, "Wow, this is hard, and I can find my way through it!"

CHAPTER 4

Connection

Title

Trade With Me?

Artist

Joanna (2012), sopho-
more in high school

Artist Notes (revised
senior year, 2014)

Inspired by *Lord of the
Flies* and its reflection on whether humans are innately good or evil,
Trade With Me? illustrates my fear of the duality of our nature. While
the extent of darkness each person casts over their secrets may vary,
everyone has a part of themselves that is parceled off from the rest of
the world. At times I fear this inner self will tire of hiding and attempt to
swap places—a prospect that is especially daunting with the amount of
scrutiny seniors receive. While this trade is unlikely to occur, the hand
in this piece represents the unavoidable connection between both sides.
The pressure to put on a good front is paramount as admissions boards
are judging prospective students while underclassmen and teachers
alike expect the senior class to serve as exemplary role models.

During our project the students developed new and important friendships with each other. Without the space and opportunities our empowerment group provided, they would not have made these friendships. In many cases, the students in our groups had taken classes and extracurricular activities together since elementary school. Despite all of the time they had spent together, they only knew each other superficially. This is an important lesson for counselors and teachers of gifted and high-achieving students. Connection does not happen by accident. The high-stakes context of high-stress programs does not always facilitate friendships organically. Therefore, schools must be proactive in creating space and opportunities for high-achieving youth to build connected peer relationships. During the years I ran the empowerment group, I identified three considerations that helped facilitate this level of connection among our students: belonging, relatedness, and closeness (see Figure 2).

Although I knew that rapport and trust were essential for YPAR projects, I did not anticipate how deeply participating in this group would matter to the students in our gifted program. Overwhelmingly, the student researchers cited the lessons they learned about relationships and the friendships they formed with each other as their most important takeaways from our project.

Belonging

As a teacher and facilitator for this project, I set norms around belonging, relatedness, and closeness. We decided that there were certain behaviors and patterns of participation that were expected in our group; these included being present, accepting our peers, practicing courage, honoring diversity, and assuming positive intent. Over time, as our community became closer, what it meant to belong to this group evolved as well. The norms we had started our group with gradually evolved into a group culture that honored our personal and collective identities, strengths, and interests.

Belonging	+ Relatedness	+ Closeness	= Connection
Being included, accepted, and recognized as an important part of the group, team, or relationship.	Sharing common interests, experiences, goals, and/or identities.	Building a shared history where it is safe to be "real" and vulnerable.	Relationships that matter (professional or personal; groups, classes, teams, 1:1).

FIGURE 2. Creating connected classes, teams, and support groups.

MY JOURNAL
Kathryn

March 2014

I carry in trays of muffins and strawberries. Ty, Flora, and Ana are already waiting even though our book discussion doesn't start for another 15 minutes. Ana jumps up and hugs me. I haven't seen her in a year. She's studying computer science at a prestigious college known for STEM programs. She's chopped off her hair. She tells me her sister doesn't like it. Her sister looks at me and rolls her eyes. I tell Ana she looks confident, which is true, although the new hairstyle may or may not be a factor in the confidence she is exuding.

Today, our group is meeting to discuss Sheryl Sandberg's book *Lean In*. Sandberg is the COO of Facebook, and her book on gender and leadership recently skyrocketed to a best seller. When I read the book last summer, I texted Ana as soon as I finished. I thought it would be interesting for her to read before her computer science internship at Facebook.

She tells me she didn't have a chance to read it before her internship, but that once she arrived at Facebook, Ms. Sandberg gave all of the women interns copies of the book and then had them over to her house to discuss.

Ana laughs, "It was the fanciest barbecue I've ever been to."

Soon a dozen young women are gathered around the table. We pass sandwiches, flatbreads, and cookies. Over the next 90 minutes we discuss leadership, gender roles, double standards, goals, and the beautiful spring weather.

Our luncheons were social-emotional tethers to our hurried school days. They brought the student groups together in ways that were uncommon in the high-stakes and high-stress advanced course and extracurricular schedule. Faith reflected,

> This project . . . has given me a group of friends that really understands some of the issues that I've gone through/ am going through more than others. All of the girls in this group are very mature for their age and very gifted, so we all tend to have similar insecurities/fears and those insecurities/fears tend to be different than [those of] most other people that I interact with. It's nice because it's very easy to look around (especially when we were in high school) and be like "what's wrong with me, why am I so different?" But in this group I have found other people who understand and I'm so grateful!

Belonging to this group was a source of comfort for all of us. The students frequently told each other that being part of the research team and/or empowerment group mattered to them.

Relatedness

Over and over again, the students told me that they had thought they were "the only" high-achieving person who was struggling to navigate the stress and pressures of school. They were constantly surprised to learn that their feelings and challenges were shared across the group. "You, too?" was a frequent question at our meetings and luncheons. It followed stories of panic attacks, insecurities, and doubts. The students shook their heads, surprised that their peers, whom they thought of as "the brightest" and "most together," also experienced these feelings. In this way, the students, like the adults at our school, were also buying into the masked affective crisis. "Oh, but she is so smart!" they sometimes told me about a particular person— never mind that the entire group was extraordinarily high-achieving and gifted. As the students learned that these experiences were neither isolated nor exclusively individual, they began to wonder what broader conditions might be contributing to their feelings of doubt and imposter syndrome.

Achievement was the first common interest, experience, and identity we shared. However, as complex human beings, we brought many identities to this project other than gender and achievement. For example, after Elaine heard Melissa's radio story on the shame and pride she felt around her Chinese heritage, Elaine reached out to say that she felt that way, too. Melissa and Elaine then talked about the ways their experiences as Vietnamese and Chinese young women were both similar and different. There was a special moment of closeness at one of our team meetings when Elaine taught Melissa how to make Vietnamese spring rolls. As they were rolling spring rolls, they swapped family peanut sauce recipes and shared stories about the similarities of their family dinners. Both young women also educated our team about the ways that their cultures, including stereotyping (and in some instances, discrimination), influenced their experiences and identities. These related experiences led to a deeper friendship between Elaine and Melissa.

Although the closeness we found through our research team was a source of comfort, it was also the beginning of a new pattern of thinking about affective development, difference, and relationships. The student researchers frequently commented on how powerful it was to learn that they were not alone in their fears, anxieties, and worries. In fact, they learned that sharing these feelings often made them less intimidating. Through talking and working as a team, we found countless reasons to connect with each other. These reasons were grounded in an empathetic attempt to try to understand each other's lived experiences.

Closeness

Through our group meetings, research projects, team-building activities, and workshops, we built a shared history where it was safe to be "real" and vulnerable. In addition to finding points in common, it was just as valuable to connect with women whose experiences and identities were different from our own. Elaine was Claudia's first openly gay friend. Faith was the first person many of the student researchers knew who had struggled with anorexia. Melissa shared powerful stories of both shame and pride about her Chinese culture. Jessica challenged our team to think more critically about the financial costs associated with high school graduation and the college application process. Whitney challenged our team to think more critically about race, in particular about what it meant to be Black and gifted.

As the student researchers transitioned to college, they looked for other communities and peer groups in which they could experience similar feelings of belonging, relatedness, and closeness. The first few weeks of college were sometimes lonely as students tried to find "their people." Heidi wrote me during her second week of college with a list of observations, including the following.

HEIDI'S JOURNAL
First-Year College Student

September 2014

I live in a hallway of 30 engineering majors . . . we've noticed that all of our friendships seem shallow, which makes the transition very difficult. At home there's friendships you've built up over years and years and are very deep and comforting. Then when you go to college (especially out of state with only a handful of kids from your hometown near campus) you suddenly don't have those deep connections near you. Technology makes it a little bit easier, but because all of my friends are scattered and busy with their lives, I've only had daily contact with one person and weekly contact with two other girls, and all have been very brief and mostly over text ("what's up?" type conversations). No one has found a great solution for this; I really think it's just time. But that might be one of the most difficult parts of college so far.

Several of the student researchers echoed Heidi's remarks and shared that they were also looking for peer groups and friendships in college. They told me that these relationships took work and intentionality. However, because of what they had learned from our research group, they were willing to make time and spend energy cultivating these relationships. They had learned how affirming and powerful connecting to a peer group could be.

The Momentum of Connection

Connection tended to gain momentum and lead to deeper relationships and new relationships. Once our research team experienced the importance of connection, they felt compelled to connect with and support more high-achieving young women outside of our group. Jessica reflected that our research

> made me more aware of how unhealthy the pressures gifted girls like us put on themselves [are], and how it doesn't have to be this way. We can do things to change the norm and help others—like how we gave the workshops at [the governor's school].

As in the workshops Jessica mentions, connection served as an impetus for several research cycles in our project. Once the student researchers found ways to support one another, they then sought out ways to connect with and support larger and more diverse communities, such as when Jessica initiated a cap and gown drive for low-income seniors. Their radio stories were another of example of this connection. Leslie shared that she hoped her radio story connected with others:

> I really do hope . . . that some of the listening audience heard our stories and became all that more aware about many of the problems facing teenage girls today. Adults can be clueless sometimes and I hope our honest dialogue opened their eyes to the truth. I do know my uncle listened to them, and even though he is an old conservative . . . he thought our stories were good.

The desire to connect more purposefully and more broadly resulted in a wide range of action projects. These projects tended to follow a pattern of (1) identifying and reflecting on a problem that mattered at a personal level, (2) planning ways to address that problem, and (3) taking action to offer solutions.

The following are some reflections on the ways Elaine saw connection "blurring lines" between people and influencing how she initiated and maintained relationships with younger students. Through track and band, Elaine took on leadership roles as she connected with her peers, particularly her younger peers. These relationships shifted Elaine's self-concept about her own ability to be a mentor or leader.

ELAINE'S JOURNAL
Senior in High School

June 2015

I never really saw myself as a mentor, to be honest, but looking back on senior year, I see many moments where I was one. . . . Being the drum major allowed me to build strong relationships and earn respect from many individuals in band, and trust developed from there. There were times when my kiddos would ask for advice whether it be in band, nerves for an audition, classes, how to approach a teacher, things going on at home, and even . . . relationships, which is actually pretty flattering that they trust me enough to come to me for guidance.

. . . I guess I was also a mentor in track as well, the more that I think about it. I did mentor B. kind of, although I never viewed it as mentoring. I just see it as a close friendship. I think with compassion many of these lines can blur, and I think that is often a value.

. . . It's a lot easier to be a mentor to those I already have a relationship with, and it feels less like I'm being a mentor, but the impact left is a lot stronger. It never hurts to be the one to reach out and lend a helping hand to those I don't know though, and I guess an impact can still be made.

Elaine credited connection as the catalyst for effective mentoring. Likewise, in our research team we saw connection as the catalyst for courage, action, and self-care. As Elaine noticed through her relationships in track, the "impact left is a lot stronger" when connections are intentionally developed and nurtured. This impact was both personal (in our personal relationships and self-care work) and public (through community action). Just as Elaine did in reflecting on her relationship with B., our research team explored the imperative roles compassion and trust played in the ways communities evolve.

Our research community neither existed nor developed in a vacuum. Instead, each of the women on our research team came to this project as part of their own communities. These additional communities of experts informed our research, inquiry, and perspectives. Elaine's band and track mates are examples of these additional communities. During the course of our project, all of these communities evolved and changed. In the following section, I explore how the high-stakes nature of high-stress schools interfered with the student researchers' ability to develop and nurture connections.

High Stress, High Schools, and (Dis)Connection

During intense periods of school stress, instead of speaking of connection, the students spoke of hurt and misunderstanding. They shared that the high-stress nature of high school, particularly during college applications and the AP testing window, was often incompatible with supportive friendships and relationships. We observed that during the most intense periods of stress, the students' relationships suffered. There were more disagreements with peers, romantic partners, and parents. There were more tears and talks of self-doubt. Unfortunately, these were the precise periods when students could have most benefited from a supportive peer group. In schools, we can anticipate when these heightened periods of stress will occur (e.g., the college applications period, finals, AP testing season, etc.) and ought to build in more social-emotional supports for students grounded in connection. The following is a conversation between Leslie and Faith, written in our collective journal during the AP testing period.

TWO-WAY JOURNAL BETWEEN LESLIE AND FAITH
Seniors in High School

April 2015

LESLIE: Ughhhhhhhhh. Lack of sleep and constant stress have been plaguing me recently. I would say I am getting about 3 to 6 hours on average, but I have been having to pull some all-nighters recently. Also I have been very stressed out about making my college decision recently. It is hard to make such a big decision, knowing it will affect the rest of my life. Additionally, I have been severely doubting my abilities recently, which definitely made selecting [an Ivy League] difficult. I didn't think I could be successful and I am not quite over that. I think that a lot of my social and emotional problems will resolve themselves once the school year ends, or at least I hope they will.

FAITH: I would say that sleep is definitely lacking right now, and I would agree that I am doubting my abilities a lot—to keep my 4.0 and excel on my AP tests. Probably more even than that I'm doubting my abilities to memorize an hour of music for my senior recital. I want to be able to be there for all of my friends' graduation parties and end senior year in a somewhat stereotypical high school way, so to speak, but at the same time that's not really possible with how much practicing I have to do, and I'm really starting to doubt my abilities.

In this conversation, Leslie discussed how the high-stress and high-stakes decisions and assessments of the end of her senior year inhibited her ability to take care of herself. (Self-care is discussed at length in Chapter 5.) As Leslie considered all of the stressors in her life and her feelings of self-doubt, she did not mention any supportive connections. Faith, who echoed many of Leslie's reflections on the lack of self-care and increasing self-doubt, did mention supportive connections: "I want to be able to be there for all of my friends." However, she added that the nature of the high-stress context made it "not really possible [to maintain these connections] with how much . . . I have to do." Although the student researchers found it difficult to maintain their personal relationships, they shared that they were grateful for the continuity of our empowerment group.

During high-stress periods, school-based interventions in courage, connection, and self-care can be important ways for students to connect, support, and share together. The students said they "counted on" our group. They credited it as the connection that "pulled them through" the precipice landscape of AP tests, the college decision process, and graduation as "happier and healthier" young women.

We knew that belonging, relatedness, and closeness were necessary for connection. However, we wondered what conditions made connection possible. Why did some groups or teams lead to real relationships, and others to superficial acquaintances? We suspected that this discrepancy had something to do with dialogue, story sharing, and the honest exchange of ideas. As I explored our notes, experiences, and data, I discovered three key conditions that were essential to the ways we built connection: critical listening, compassion, and communication (see Figure 3). In the following section, I discuss how these conditions worked together.

Critical Listening, Compassion, and Communication

In my first proposal for this research project, I wrote about the importance of voice. At that time, I thought that voice was analogous to agency and authorship. As a YPAR researcher, I was committed to making certain that the student researchers' ideas were central to the study. As our specific project unfolded, however, I noticed that we were also attending to and valuing each other's voices in a literal way. In addition to focusing on agency and authorship (as I had planned), I found that we were also paying attention to audio and nonverbals through critical listening (which I had not considered). In fact, critical listening was so essential to connection in our group that it is repeated twice in the definition in Figure 3, once on its own and again as a condition for effective communication.

79

Critical Listening	+ Compassion	+ Communication	= Connection
Carefully attending to verbal and nonverbal cues.	Showing concern, warmth, and empathy.	Using critical listening to reflect, respond, and dialogue.	Relationships where members trust each other, problem solve, collaborate, and offer reciprocal support.

FIGURE 3. Facilitating meaningful and effective relationships.

MY JOURNAL
Kathryn

Spring 2015

On a Roundtable Dialogue

In a classroom large enough to hold 100 students, the six of us pull desks so close together they are touching. I have prepared a few topics for us to cover. We talk about social-emotional needs, gender, self-care, hopes, and fears. The students are honest; as usual, they practice courage in a way that inspires me. There are moments when they are uncertain. There are times when they sound young. There are times when they disagree. . . . We talk at length about fears as the students ready themselves for college. On this topic there is little disagreement; everyone is worried about failure: "I am afraid I've fooled everyone and that I actually can't do it." Everyone nods in quiet agreement. I think about all I have read on imposter phenomenon.

The tape runs for more than an hour. Sometimes voices break, other times we laugh loudly. I am thrilled to have these sounds, the humanizing audio of our team, preserved on tape.

Throughout the roundtable, the students practiced both reflective expression, by drawing on their personal experiences and challenges, as well as the critical listening covered in the previous section. The learning process that happened between what we shared (often courageously) and what we heard (through critical listening) led to deeper connections and new knowledge. That is, personal stories brought us closer together, and reflecting on those personal experiences in a community allowed us to posit new ideas about identity, gender, the college transition, and affective development.

When I first observed that our research team was paying attention to the variance in our voices, I attributed this to our workshops on radio storytelling. I assumed we were simply utilizing a new tool in our storytelling repertoire. However, the more we talked about critical listening as a research team, the more I realized that the reason our voices mattered to us was not only because of the radio lessons on sound; it was also our care and concern for each other that gave these voices value. In short, our voices mattered to us because the people on our research team mattered to us.

Our dialogues, laughter, tears, and whispers were additional details we collected as we cataloged the development of our community. We noticed the ways laughter could bring people together. We paid attention to the times voices broke from sadness and used this as a signal that more compassion might be needed. Being able to identify these nuances facilitated even deeper relationships.

Effective communication is the practice of using critical listening to reflect, respond, and dialogue with others. We engaged in communication and reflective expression in many forms throughout our project, including writing, speaking, composing, singing, and texting. The topics covered in our meetings and dialogues included great breadth and depth. Although we had many common experiences, we also had many different experiences. Our early generalizations were almost always either misguided or insufficient. Over time our team learned to stop generalizing and start listening. Instead of either/or assumptions (e.g., either Asian or athletic), we discovered that people are both/and (e.g., both high-achieving and insecure).

Within our project, compassion included showing concern, warmth, and empathy. As our community developed, each of our unique voices became familiar, and hearing them garnered a warm emotional response. There is sentimentality in attending to these audio details, similar to the way we collected photos during our project. As previously mentioned, the high-stress nature of high schools often made carving out time for meaningful connection challenging. However, as an educator, I believe the benefits of listening to young people far outweigh the logistical challenges needed to make that happen. Our research project required regular team meetings. In the regularity of those meeting, we learned about the ways connection develops and how a consistent peer group can serve as a powerful student support.

Connection Is Complicated

Connection is not always linear, simple, or smooth. More often it is complicated, messy, and challenging. Although we experienced acceptance, compassion, and celebration, we also experienced contention, disagreement, and hurt. As the student researchers emotionally invested in each other (e.g., disclosing sensitive stories, developing deeper friendships, and seeing each other during vulnerable times), they found that in addition to offering deeper support, their relationships with each other also became higher risk. Caring and relationship building are vulnerable experiences. There were sometimes challenges and points of a disagreement in our research team. The following is a journal excerpt I wrote after a conversation with Leslie.

MY JOURNAL
Kathryn

May 2015

Leslie is back from AP Bio. She's the second student to return from the exam. The first shared that the test was harder than everyone expected. Leslie has tears in her eyes and a bag of Taco Bell in her hand. I offer her jokes, chocolate, and tissues. She says "yes" to the tissues. Someone asks if she is upset about bio. She says, "It's not that."

Another student and I offer to dance for her. The student elbows me in my ribs and jokes, "You can't keep up with me!"

At this point, Leslie starts to cry. The student stops joking immediately and asks if Leslie would like some of her gluten-free cheesecake. Leslie shakes her head.

I give Leslie some space and go back to my desk to work. When she finishes her tacos, she comes over. I ask if she would like to go on a walk. She says "yes."

It is sunny and windy outside. We talk about biology. It didn't go well. She didn't finish. There was an error in timing that got resolved, but it "threw her off." The proctors forgot to check calculators, but scientific calculators weren't allowed, so the students who used those had to have a note sent in with their tests. I ask her if her AP score matters. It doesn't. As a biology major she thinks she should probably take biology at her [Ivy League] college. She says, "It is just embarrassing." We keep walking.

I don't want to press her, so I ask her about Mother's Day. I am aware that we have walked quite a distance from school. We turn right to make a large loop. There is park and Leslie suggests we cut across it. She tells me there is something she wants to talk about, but she is afraid she will cry.

I tell her, "It's not a big deal. I cry, too."

"What if I cry so hard, you can't understand me?"

"I am a pretty proficient translator."

She smiles. She tells me that she and Melissa spent all day Saturday studying at the public library. Then Claudia called to see if they wanted to do a bio study session at her house. She said she was worried about how productive it would be, but they decided to go. She said it started off alright. They got a pizza and were all working. She tells me that she is a very visual learner, so she needed to look at everything, not just hear it. She said she was getting distracted, so she moved into a corner by herself to focus.

Her friends made fun of her. She told me she doesn't think her friend group builds each other up, that instead they "are all so competitive and really make fun of each other when someone doesn't get something." She thinks this is contributing to her self-doubt.

She tells me, "I felt so horrible when I realized that. Then I got a migraine."

She called her dad to pick her up. She woke up to a group text initiated by her boyfriend, who was part of the study group. He said he was sending this text on behalf of the group to say she had been very immature.

She wants to know what to do with her friends. She wants to know what to do with her boyfriend. She tells me her boyfriend said he would be a horrible school counselor, because if anyone came to him with a problem, he would just tell that person to "get over it." She says he never talks about feelings.

Instead of walking toward school, we find ourselves walking around a lake behind the park. I tell her that it must be hard to go through that. She nods and then asks if I see the goslings. I don't at first and then I notice a few little birds, so young their feathers still look fuzzy. We've come upon a whole gaggle of geese. Leslie snaps a photo with her phone. We tiptoe closer together. There are dozens of little goslings; they are everywhere. One of the grown geese stares us down directly. I imagine she is the mother goose. Another bird catches my eye though. She stands apart looking at us from her periphery and then pretending to look away. Something about her demeanor is familiar; she is protecting in her own way. She stands tall, aware of each gosling, but uncertain in the best course of action. Leslie and I try to count them, but there are too many. Suddenly a large group takes to the water and they glide away across the lake.

Leslie experienced hurt and misunderstanding by her friend group and boyfriend. These were some of the people she cared the most deeply for, and when they did not support or understand her in the ways she had expected or needed, she felt isolated and confused. As Leslie and I talked about these relationships, we discussed the conditions of how connection is established and maintained. Leslie used communication, compassion, and critical listening to repair and improve her relationship with her friend group. She tried to use these same strategies with her boyfriend, but continued to feel unheard and unsupported. A week before she left for college, they broke up.

Teachers who work closely with young people, particularly around affective needs, navigate uncertain terrain. For me, these complications included not always knowing the best ways to offer guidance, support, or counsel students. I used critical listening, compassion, and communication as a compass for navigating these situations. All relationships are reciprocal; although I served as a counselor, teacher, and facilitator, the student researchers also taught me countless lessons. In particular, I learned more about youth culture, social-emotional needs, and the pressures of high-stress and high-stakes schools.

Near the end of our project, I confided in the student researchers that I was nervous about taking on my new position as Director of Academic Affairs. I told the research team that I was drawing on our lessons around courage at a precipice to take this leap into educational administration. Faith said, "That's so fantastic! I'm so proud of you . . . I know you most definitely have the courage to take this leap in stride." Normalizing doubt and using courage and connection to find our way through doubt was a critical takeaway from our research project. Students need to affirm that (1) their feelings are valid, (2) we all encounter scary challenges, and (3) there are social-emotional tools we can use to find our way through these challenges.

Mothers: Mentors and Critics

Although not within the original scope of our research activities, the relationships we had with our mothers were connections that directly shaped our sensemaking processes and many of our understandings about what it means to be young women. Collectively we came from many different kinds of households: women-headed homes, homes with mother breadwinners, egalitarian homes, and traditional patriarchal households. Culture played a role in some of the relationships student researchers had with their mothers. For instance, Melissa talked to the group about "tiger mothers" (Chua, 2011), a phrase that refers to the extreme intensity, pressure, and emotional distance that Westerners sometimes perceive in Chinese mothers. Melissa's relationship with her mother was the most complicated mother-daughter relationship for our research team to understand. She shared stories of shame, fear, and intensity. And yet, even as her mother did things that infuriated or hurt her, their connection was one of the most important connections in her life. She loves her mother deeply.

MELISSA'S NOTE TO THE RESEARCH TEAM
Senior in High School

Spring 2015

This sounds bad . . . but my family would definitely [say] the things we talk about [in our YPAR team] are soft or weak. Like the power of vulnerability and stuff is very much a Western way of thinking. And sometimes I feel stifled because I've always been taught that you should keep your negative aspects within the family. And when I seek support outside of my family I always think: What reason do these strangers have to support me? And I feel like I'm almost betraying my family. There's this Chinese concept called "losing face" that encompasses your personal image and how others perceive you as strong or weak or whatever. This is pretty personal, but most of you know: I got child services called on me and my mom, and the kickback from that was not great from my family. Sometimes I really hate the "Chinese" form of support. I know my family would do anything for me, but there's just an entirely new set of permissibility than what I've been taught here, and it's difficult to reconcile the two. All of this makes it difficult to accept or reach for support.

Although Melissa embraced the themes of our study, particularly our work on courage and vulnerability, her family and cultural background led to internal tensions about key project concepts, including affective education and wholeheartedness. The connections Melissa maintained and valued with both her family and our research team were important in shaping the ways she navigated the transition from high school to college, her own struggles with mental health and wellness, and her personal beliefs about strength and vulnerability.

Melissa saw her mother as both her central critic and central mentor. As we dug deeper, we found this to be true of almost all of the mother-daughter relationships in our research team. Often the student researchers talked about their mothers as the voice in their head. In our team meetings we discussed the importance of self-talk. As we evaluated the ways we spoke to ourselves, we found that often the voice and messages we heard in our heads came from conversations we had with our mothers. Like all of the relationships discussed in this chapter, the ways we connected with our mothers were complicated. Although the student researchers spoke of their mothers using terms like *proud*, *loving*, and *supportive*, they also spoke of worry, pressure, and disappointment. For example, Leslie shared,

> My relationship with my mother is complex and complicated, but I love her more than anything and I know she feels the same way. She always calls me "her greatest accomplishment," which quite honestly I feel is unfair to my brother, but it is the sentiment that counts. I wouldn't trade the world for my mom, and I will be extremely lucky if I turn out to be half as wonderful as she is.

The student researchers shared that they knew their mothers worried about them when they were at school, social events, and extracurricular activities. Their fathers certainly worried, too; however, these relationships did not come up nearly as often in our dialogues. The student researchers frequently said they needed to call, text, or check in with their mothers to process situations and share news before going to an activity, or if they were running late. Although they sometimes seemed annoyed at having to check in with their mothers so frequently, they all confided that they were scared to leave their mothers when they left for college. Elaine shared the following journal with our team in the collective journal.

ELAINE'S JOURNAL
Senior in High School

June 2015

I LOVE MY MOMMY! She's the best. I think it's funny how everyone posts on social media that they have the best mom in the world because little do they know that I actually have the best mom in the world. Lol, but forreal [sic], I'm kind of afraid to leave my mom here when I go to college. She's always worrying about me, even when I'm out in broad daylight doing something school related. I hate being out knowing my mom is worried sick. I did write her a poem for Mother's Day. Here are a few stanzas from it:

You have always been a role model in my life,
And have taught me so much.
I can't imagine leaving for college,
I'm going to miss your hugs and gentle touch.

I want to make you proud,
And make you say, "That's my baby."
I finna [fixing to] graduate from [university] with a 4.0,
And prove that I'm a well put-together young lady.

But mom please don't worry about me,
Because I know you always do.
I'll always be your little girl,
I'll always be Elaine Pho.

In a few short stanzas Elaine explains how her deep connection with her mother is marked by love, affection, and worry. She also shares the pressure she feels to make her mother proud. Elaine speaks about the tension between her mother's identity as a woman compared to her own identity as a woman. She mentions wanting to prove she's "a well put-together young lady." Elaine's personal style is casual and athletic; she prefers sporting clothes and ponytails, and does not wear makeup. However, for her high school graduation events, her mother bought her dresses and did her hair and makeup. At baccalaureate and commencement, I heard several students and faculty remark that they did not recognize Elaine.

Elaine also influenced her mother. Elaine shared that in the weeks before she left for college, her mother asked her for guidance on strength training. Elaine worked with her to begin a weight-lifting regimen. During her senior year, Elaine experienced an award-winning track season, was severely injured twice, came out as gay to her parents, and chose her college and potential career path. These were emotional experiences, and through all of them Elaine counted on her mother for support. Her relationship with her mother was grounded in closeness, relatedness, and belonging. They loved each other completely and tried to understand each other's lived experiences, both those that were similar (e.g., being Vietnamese women and valuing the same family-specific traditions) and those that were different (e.g., their ages and the ways they performed their gender identities).

Claudia was a bit quieter during our discussions on mothers. On the afternoon of her final one-on-one dialogue for our research project, I asked her about her relationship with her mother. To my surprise, she started weeping:

> Well . . . Most of my family is very well educated, but my mom . . . She did well in high school and then she took one community college class and flunked out and that's it. So . . . I know she's given up a lot for me. I also know she is so proud of me. And I don't think I've ever told her how much that means to me.

It was difficult for Claudia to get through this as she was crying. We sat together on the couch in my living room. When she was ready, we talked some more. I did not press Claudia with follow-up questions. Claudia seemed to feel personal guilt about her mother's life path. She shared that she and her father (an engineer) sometimes "looked down" on her mother. As she and I talked, it was obvious that Claudia was having a difficult time processing this realization.

Claudia told me that the other students' stories about their mothers caused her to reconsider her own relationship with her mother. She identified a gap in connection and made plans to intervene. While we visited, Claudia was in a large, hard cast that covered her shoulder and arm. Because Claudia wasn't able to drive with the cast, her mother dropped her off and later picked her up. A couple of weeks later, Claudia was moving into an apartment a few minutes away from her college campus. Her mother planned to go to school with her for the first month or so to help Claudia acclimate to the new apartment and college and take care of her as she healed from surgery. As we talked, Claudia told me she planned to use that time more intentionally to build a stronger connection with her mother.

I followed up with Claudia a few weeks later to see how she and her mother were doing in her new apartment. Claudia told me her mother was teaching her how to cook and that they were enjoying "lots of movie nights." She sounded very happy.

Connectedness as a Catalyst for Action

As Elaine demonstrated in her journal on mentoring younger students (see p. 76), we often saw connection as a catalyst for action. The student researchers spoke of mentoring younger students and supporting friends who were struggling with mental health, the college process, or other challenges. The student researchers were eager to share the lessons they had learned and the strategies they discovered through our research project. The more connected the students became, the more interested they were in connecting with people on a broader scale. As our project continued, the student researchers planned workshops on health and wellness, organized clothing drives, and engaged in more public projects with broader and more diverse communities. The following is an excerpt from one of Leslie's college essays that speaks of the meaning she found in connecting with others through service.

EXCERPT FROM ONE OF LESLIE'S COLLEGE ESSAYS

November 2014

What does it mean to "lead a meaningful life?" Do I have to cure cancer or mediate a peace agreement between warring countries? I do not think so. I believe that making a difference, no matter how small, is creating meaning and purpose to one's existence. . . . I must seek out every opportunity I can to make someone's day better, but I also cannot beat myself up when I fail to see the impact I have made. I engage in community service because I know that I would feel eternally hungry if I did not attempt to make the world a better place. . . . I want to be able to wake up in the morning and know that if I died today, I would be satisfied with my contributions to the world and its people. I cannot wait until tomorrow to give back to my community, I must do everything I can today to make a change, thus leading a meaningful life.

During this project we practiced many ways to make a difference. There were several research cycles of observing, reflecting, planning, and then taking action to support our peers, communities, networks, and groups. We learned that there are many affective outcomes of engaging in community action, including becoming more confident and connected. As Leslie suggested in her essay, "making a difference, no matter how small" is what leads to a "meaningful life."

Jessica told me,

> To me, being an activist means that when you see a problem you try to do something to change it and make the situation better. That can come in many different forms, like raising awareness, volunteering, raising funds, etc. I do consider myself an activist.

Addressing poverty has always been a passion of Jessica's. This is the young woman who spearheaded a grant-writing effort to subsidize the costs of summer programming for low-income youth, raising more than $1,000 as a 16-year-old. I know much of this interest is personal; her parents expected her to pay all of her college expenses herself. The ways this financial reality limited her postsecondary options became a catalyst for Jessica to take action. The following is an example of one of the ways Jessica used her own experiences to connect with her graduating class and initiate greater access for her peers.

MY JOURNAL
Kathryn

Graduation Day 2015

It is a few hours before the commencement ceremony. My phone dings. It is Jessica.

> JESSICA: I had an idea to do a cap and gown donation drive. That way people who can't afford it will only have to buy the tassel. What do you think? If you like the idea, I was thinking we could set up a box in the [gifted resource]

room and people could stop by next week. And I'll put out info before graduation on people's seats and maybe make an announcement.

KATHRYN: Love it! Run it by [the assistant principal] tonight. I'm thrilled to help.

JESSICA: Great! I will make up some info sheets and email [the assistant principal]. Thanks!

. . . Later at commencement, I pin Jessica's white collar onto her gown. She shows me her large stack of announcements advertising the cap and gown drive. I smile and then watch as she weaves through all of the chairs, leaving an announcement on each seat, seemingly oblivious to the flurry of hugs, tears, and graduation gowns.

Back-to-School Update

I am cleaning out my classroom, readying it for the school year and a new division chair. A few tears catch in my throat as I pack up cards and letters from my students. I think about the student researchers also packing up their rooms for college. I notice the big gray tub that Jessica brought in her for her cap and gown drive. I sigh. I was surprised that it wasn't a bigger success. Then I look closer and notice the lid is ajar. The tub is completely filled with caps and gowns. When did we get so many more? I do some investigating and find that another announcement went out over social media, and the response was enthusiastic.

Jessica used the tools we developed through our research, including observing, reflecting, planning, and acting, in order to initiate a cap and gown drive. She observed and experienced the ways that financial scarcity limited her own college options. She was frequently struck by how expensive the transition process from high school to college was. From testing fees (AP, SAT, ACT), to college application fees, to cap and gown fees, to the expenses associated with prom, it seemed that everywhere Jessica turned, there was another expense. She brought this up in our team meetings and wanted to do something that would help. Connecting with our research team gave her the self-efficacy to know that she could do something to make a difference. The cap and gown drive was her solution. Working with the communication tools we refined throughout this project, including written announcements, text messaging, and social media, she orchestrated a drive to help eliminate the cap and gown cost for low-income seniors.

An Exercise in Hope

Connecting as a research team had a profound positive impact on all of us. Although our experiences were influenced by our individual positionalities, we collectively forged new relationships, practiced courage, and took action to improve the health and wellness outcomes of high-achieving women (including ourselves). We discovered that connection and activism are closely related and bound together by hope. Our research team believed that through connecting with others, we could contribute to positive change. When reflecting on our storytelling work, Leslie shared,

> I think stories are one of the most compelling forms of media that there is because it really allows you to be empathetic and understand people in a way that, you know, other forms of media can't. And that's something I've learned with this project and with the research team . . . and I just love the way that stories and sharing honestly and vulnerably can really connect people and form a community.

When I was young, my grandmother taught me the Hebrew phrase *Tikkun Olam*, which literally translates to "world repair." However, it is used more colloquially as: to heal, repair, and transform, or to engage in social justice. It was easy to see how my grandmother lived this principle in her own work as a civil rights and feminist activist. In recent years, Tikkun Olam has become popularized in American culture (Salovey, 2015) and in teaching (Block, 2008).

During our research project, Yale president Peter Salovey (2015) delivered a baccalaureate speech urging his graduate students to also practice Tikkun Olam:

> What I am going to suggest to you today . . . is that your purpose in life as a graduate from Yale is simply this: to improve the world. In the Jewish tradition this is called *Tikkun Olam*, literally *to repair the world*. . . . Go forth from this place with grateful hearts, paying back the gift you have received here

by paying it forward for others. Find that part of the world
that feels chipped or bent or broken—and commit yourself,
once again, to Tikkun Olam. (para. 7, 18)

In many ways, connection is the act of healing, repair, and transformation. Throughout our project, we saw our own ability to heal, repair, and transform ourselves, our peer groups, and even our larger communities. With connection as a foundation, the student researchers were able to take courageous risks, many of which led to deeper and more honest relationships, as well as to action projects that supported the communities they cared about. The student researchers inspired me, as my grandmother did, for their ability to take action against injustice and hurt. The student researchers tackled sexism, homophobia, poverty, and mental health stigma. These young women had the faith to imagine a more just world and the courage to begin making that vision a reality. As an educational leader, I believe world repair is possible through student leadership, the dynamic possibility of connection, and the power of our collective imagination.

CHAPTER 5

Self-Care

Title

A Measure of Value

Artist

Samantha Ding (2014), senior in high school

Artist Notes

This piece speaks to the great emphasis that young people, especially girls, place on weight and measurements to determine their value as a person. Body image can take over one's perception of self, and often there is an overwhelming pressure to look a certain way.

This chapter was hard to write. In order to honestly report on the lessons we learned through this research, I had to admit several instances when I had been wrong, misinformed, or naive about the nature of self-care for high-achieving young women in general, and the needs of my students in particular. When I think back to the beginning of this project, I am embarrassed about how I thought we could keep our conversations about self-care at a "safe distance" from anything "too personal." I thought we would talk and read about self-care abstractly, discussing generalized experiences of high-achieving or gifted women. This proved to be an absurd assumption.

Through this research, I learned that self-care required personal reflection, dialogue, and disclosure. I didn't expect to open up about parenting, grieving, or stress. Yet sharing these feelings became an important turning point for me. In these instances, the student researchers taught me how deeply embedded the masked affective crisis is for gifted women, including, I reluctantly admitted, myself. The students taught me that masking pain, by ignoring it, hiding it in sweeping generalizations, or shutting off dialogues around it, is incompatible with healing or self-care. They modeled that, yes, talking about difficult and personal topics, such as depression, doubt, and hurt, requires tremendous courage. However, again and again, we discovered that courage is almost always rewarded with deeper and more meaningful connections, healing, and growth.

Self-Care Stories From Barnwood High School

When I took the position to chair Barnwood's gifted department, our highest achieving high school juniors were in the throes of a self-care crisis. Although this crisis had been building for some time, the adults at school had failed to notice the signs until they reached alarming proportions. Navigating this crisis was my initiation into teaching in gifted education. Because of this, I closely associate social-emotional needs with gifted education. The emphasis on high-stress academic programs can often feel incompatible with developing and nurturing self-care. We need to restructure schools so that young people understand that achievement and self-care are not mutually exclusive endeavors. Instead, they are reciprocal elements for a holistically successful life. In this chapter, I share how our group

96

navigated the nuances of self-care at Barnwood and the lessons we learned about the importance of engaging in this work in schools.

Self-care topics, including mental health, panic attacks, unhealthy relationships, grieving, and disordered eating, are highly charged. Teachers seldom receive training in how to navigate these topics or administrative encouragement to explore them with students. The fact that we aren't talking about these topics in our classrooms doesn't make them less real. In fact, the opposite may be true; our silence around self-care is exacerbating the need for it.

When she first joined our research team in 2014, Leslie told me,

> Lack of self-care is definitely one of my biggest weaknesses. I think I put my physical and emotional wellbeing and health at the bottom of my priorities. I feel obligated to fulfill my academic and family responsibilities before I tend to myself.

Several of the students talked about this same struggle and traced it to our larger conversations about gender and achievement. Leslie continued,

> Oftentimes, there is just not enough time in the day for me to exercise and sleep enough. Additionally, when I get stressed I tend to eat less healthy food, which is a habit that needs to stop. For me, I get in my head that I have to be successful and my definition of success, unfortunately, does not have self-care in it.

Leslie's reflections on "physical and emotional wellbeing and health" were paramount to how our team framed self-care. Working with a guidance counselor at Barnwood, we defined *self-care* as intentional practices to relieve physical, emotional, and mental stress in order to promote personal health and wellness. The ways this definition manifested across our lived experiences were highly individualized and dynamic. In Part I, I discussed how despite their accolades and accomplishments, the student researchers often did not consider themselves "successes." Leslie's reflection points to an additional disconnect she felt between being successful (which she wanted to be, but did not think she was) and practicing self-care (which she wanted to do, but did not think she had time for). Throughout our project, Leslie and the other student researchers worked to bridge this disconnect. Just as Leslie commented that she felt "obligated to fulfill my academic and family responsibilities before I tend to myself," the other student researchers described the tension between high academic achievement and self-care as a constant struggle throughout our project.

Our empowerment group became an important school-based intervention in recentering self-care. Our research team sometimes worried that sharing our struggles with self-care would jeopardize the community we were building. Thankfully, time and again, we found the opposite to be true. The more honestly and courageously we opened up about our struggles (and triumphs), the deeper our connection to each other became. As our connection to each other and our comfort with being courageous developed, so did our willingness and ability to engage in self-care. We found that self-care improved health, wellness, and achievement, and also that it had the power to amplify our other themes of courage and connection. However, making space for a self-care practice both inside and outside of school continued to be a challenge.

FAITH'S JOURNAL
Senior in High School

March 2015

Self-care is definitely hard. I am still not over my "I must exercise every day" thing. It's more of a compulsion that's a side effect of still fighting anorexia. So I wake up every morning (by 5 at the latest) and exercise for at least an hour. . . . I'm also still pretty much eating the exact same thing every day . . . but I know that I won't be able to continue eating like this every day at [college] and that thought stresses me out. I also occasionally cut back whenever I'm stressed out, which is bad because that's a slippery slope.

And I still definitely have a distorted body image of myself. Yoga was helping for a while, but I don't really have time to do it anymore with everything going on, so I've pretty much gone back to daily stress and body image insecurities (I'm fat, not pretty enough, etc.). I need to really work on chilling out. I get in my head the idea that I have to be "perfect" [but] not only is that impossible and not a good goal, my idea of perfection (specifically in body image) is very distorted because of anorexia, so that leads me to unhealthy behavior.

June 2015

Self-care does mean being physically fit and healthy, and that is extremely important to maintain as we grow up and are exposed to new things. At the same time, however, I think most people's definition of self-care focuses too much on the physical and not enough on the mental aspects. Being healthy and well means being confident in yourself and your abilities. It means loving yourself, regardless of other people's feelings toward you. It means pushing yourself and not allowing yourself to become lazy, but at the same time recognizing when something is too much and being okay with treating yourself or relaxing. Health and wellness is being satisfied with who you are . . . you have to learn to be accepting of who you are.

Faith echoes many of the concerns shared by Leslie and others on our research teams, namely that the high-stress conditions of the high-stakes transition to college often acted as a barrier to self-care. This was true even when the student researchers recognized that there were physical and emotional consequences of forgoing self-care (including, as Faith mentioned, exacerbating stress levels). Although there were many common factors in self-care work, including nutrition, mental health, exercise, positive peer group, and sleep, the particulars of each student's self-care journey were varied and personal. For example, Faith's battle with anorexia framed her self-care goals differently than Melissa's challenges with depression.

Self-Care Through Courage and Connection

Our lessons around self-care had a profound impact on me professionally and personally. The following is a note I shared with the student researchers on how our lessons around self-care influenced me. I remember feeling uncomfortable sharing this note with our student research team. Just like the students, I worried that sharing these personal challenges might change the students' impression of me.

NOTE TO THE 2015 STUDENT RESEARCH TEAM
Kathryn

April 2015

This has been an emotionally challenging period for me. My aunt passed away earlier this month. My dog was just diagnosed with cancer. My son is having a hard time finding his place at Barnwood. All semester I have been back and forth with my committee defending this research project. It's a lot on the heart. I don't talk about these things at school, because I don't always think it is appropriate for teachers to share heartache with their students. However, as a research team, I know one of our aims is to practice strong vulnerability together. Therefore, I think it is important to share some of these things.

I am noticing that my response to these kinds of challenges is changing. I think this is because of our work on affective education. As I have tackled these hard and/or heart-heavy things, I've noticed that I am looking for ways to continue to practice self-care. Some days I recognize that I need to listen to a nice song and sip a cup of tea, or take three deep breaths. I make a great effort not to stay up past 11:00 p.m., and many nights I am in bed by 10:00 p.m. I am walking and jogging a lot. I make sure I am eating fruits and vegetables and am trying to eat more protein. I schedule in quality time with my family. I pray. I reach out to friends. I evaluate my self-talk and check to see if I am being patient and kind with myself.

After I posted this note to our collective journals, the student researchers responded, not with judgment, but with compassion and support. Again and again my research pointed to these two truths:
1. Challenge and crisis are inherent to the human condition.
2. Honest and vulnerable story sharing strengthens communities and relationships.

I continued to track these lessons on self-care when the student researchers went on to college. During her first few months of college, Heidi wrote me regularly with updates on how she was translating the lessons of our empowerment group to her college experiences. As an engineering student, she approached this process with a scientific lens.

HEIDI'S JOURNAL
First-Year College Student

September 2014

Quick update on a new thing I'm trying. I found myself not taking the time to take care of me so I've decided to start a project this week. Every day I have to pick one thing to do that will improve my mind, body, or soul. Then I get to write it down in my planner in a little check box. Examples are:

> For mind: watch a TEDtalk, read a poem or short story, or learn something new

> For body: do a quick 10–15 min. workout in my room, yoga or breathing exercises, or eating an extra helping of veggies at a meal

> For soul: record what I'm thankful for, a relaxation exercise, finding a joke or inspirational quote.

I'm thinking I'll challenge my mom and maybe my roommate to join me in this endeavor. I'll keep you posted on how/if it helps.

Update January 2015

For about a month I remembered to do something to improve my mind, body, or soul almost every day. It was a good experience and I think I'll try something like it again, but it did take a lot of conscious effort and a little bit of time, so when midterms hit hard I let it drop and never found the time to restart again. However some of the habits stuck throughout the semester even when I was busy. I did try to read an article or watch a TED talk when I had a few minutes of downtime in the middle of the day. I also did yoga and deep breathing exercises whenever I got headaches, which was fairly frequently during weeks with lots of tests.

Positive Self-Image + Self-Efficacy = Preconditions for Self-Care

I often saw the relationship between self-image, self-efficacy, and self-care come to a head during senior year of high school. Senior year is a pivotal and challenging year for high-achieving students. Each year, I worked with students as they submitted college applications, prepared for AP exams, waited on financial aid and scholarship news, and finally made their college decisions. The students in our group often spoke of panic attacks during this year. Jessica told me this story about her panic attack:

> I started panicking about failing my test and then losing my 4.0 and whatnot, and just in general realizing all the stress I'd been under and I started crying and my heart was beating crazy fast and I was uncontrollably gasping for breath. . . . Anyway, that lasted over an hour before I could finally calm down. But I didn't have time for that because I had to study, so I just showered and started reviewing Calc during it [the panic attack] at like 3 in the morning. And I was just thinking, "Wow, I'm a mess."

Jessica's story illustrates some of the challenges inherent in practicing self-care in the high-stakes and high-stress context of high school. Jessica clearly recognized that she was not well: "Wow, I'm a mess." However, she believed that the pressures to maintain her GPA in her rigorous coursework, including university-level math, superseded the importance of practicing self-care by doing things like taking a break or getting enough sleep. Prior to our research project, Jessica had not considered or practiced any social-emotional strategies to respond to extreme stress. Further, she had never considered that her physical or emotional health might be as important (or more so) than achieving at high levels in school. During our research, we saw the ways overachievement and stress can mask the need for students to develop self-care practices.

Faith shared that the high-stress high school environment contributed to debilitating "self-hate" (her term):

> I hate myself for having anorexia and not being strong enough to be completely over it yet (even though I know

that would be an unreasonably fast time frame of recovery), but then I also hate myself for eating because in the weird eating-disordered part of my brain, eating feels like giving up. Obviously none of this stuff is logical, and so then I hate myself for not being logical enough.

There is a big emotional weight that teachers and counselors carry as they listen and help young people process these feelings and experiences. I wanted Faith to know that she could always come to me and share these feelings. She continued:

Anyway basically this leads to days where I sit and try to study for hours, and everything goes in through my eyes and goes completely uncoded by my brain because I can't focus. It's awful and then I hate myself because I can't study and I feel like I'm being lazy.

During her recovery, Faith frequently spoke to me about a friction between her self-care goals and overachievement culture. As a group, we attempted to recenter self-care as both an antidote and response to this overachievement culture. Students need to know who they are and believe that they are capable of working through challenges in order to practice self-care. Figure 4 outlines the ways self-image and self-efficacy work together to create the preconditions for self-care.

Rejection

The college and scholarship application process was often the student researchers' first experience with rejection. Faith told me, "The whole [college applications] process really wrecked what little self-confidence I had. Logically I do understand it's a crapshoot. It's just hard to make your heart feel what your brain knows is true."

Faith applied to eight schools and was accepted to four. Despite the acceptances, she viewed the four rejections as an affront to her worthiness as a student. Faith was not alone in this response. During the course of our study, all of the student researchers experienced rejection as a result of the college and scholarship decision process, and it was hard not to take these

Positive Self-Image	+ Self-Efficacy	= Preconditions for Self-Care
Seeing yourself (beliefs, abilities, identities) as unique and worthwhile.	The beliefs you have about your ability to solve problems, accomplish goals, and persevere through challenge.	The social and psychological conditions needed for personal health and wellness, including intentional practices to relieve physical, emotional, and mental stress.
Who am I?	Can I do challenging things?	Why and how should I take care of myself?

FIGURE 4. Preconditions for self-care.

rejections personally. Too often the students saw these rejections as affirming their self-doubts. Jessica shared,

> I had to face rejection several times—getting waitlisted to W., not getting the D. scholarship I needed. Like I've heard people say a couple of times, it was the first real rejection I'd faced growing up. I mean, I'd been rejected before—I got cut from the eighth-grade basketball team—but this was the first time it actually mattered in the long run. So yeah, it sucked.

Rejections are nearly inevitable for students who apply to select colleges and scholarships, yet the student researchers told me that they felt high school did little to help them prepare for or process rejection. Without social-emotional tools to process rejection, this became a particularly vulnerable time for the student researchers to forgo self-care, or worse, for self-harm behaviors to resurface.

Making College Decisions

Self-doubt directly impeded the student researchers' ability to both make their college decisions and feel confident after they had done so. The following is a partial transcript of reflections from Melissa's conflicted college decisions process.

CONVERSATION EXCERPTS WITH MELISSA
Kathryn

May 4, 2015

Melissa says, "Here is my dilemma. What I want to do is go to Taiwan [on study abroad] next year and then go to [our state university]. But I can't just tell my parents that I am going to do what I want to do." She is talking to Claudia.

Melissa was accepted to a selective gap year program in Taiwan and an accelerated BA/MD program. Claudia asks her if she is certain she wants to be a doctor. Melissa loves medicine but isn't completely sure. Melissa is worried about telling her mom she wants to go to Taiwan. Claudia recommends preparing a "multipoint presentation."

Melissa starts crying.

May 5, 2015

Melissa asks if we can talk in the "crying room." I grab a box of tissues. It's 10:00 a.m. and has already been an emotional day in the gifted center.

Melissa takes a deep breath, "I'm going to turn down [the BA/MD program]."

I ask her how she is feeling overall. She isn't sure.

I ask her how she is feeling about Taiwan. She is excited. She tells me her parents think that if she doesn't go to the BA/MD program, she shouldn't go to medical school at all. She is now talking about a Ph.D. in chemistry. I tell her I know she has many paths she can take and be successful with. She accepts the Taiwan study abroad and begins making calls to defer her scholarships to the state university.

May 6, 2015

Melissa comes into the gifted room early in the morning. She's not a morning person. It is obvious she has been crying. I give her a hug. We don't hug often.

"I changed my mind," she tells me. "I did a complete 180."

"Did you talk to your mom?"

"Yeah, and my sisters . . . my whole family."

I ask what I can do. We sit in two chairs near my desk. I ask her how she is feeling.

"I don't know."

"How are you feeling about [the BA/MD program]?"

"Good," she says, "even though I am crying."

We laugh. She tells me it is "the right choice." That it will be hard, but that she can do it. She says 6 years (the length of the program) isn't that long. She says Taiwan and [the state university] were the "easy way and more fun route, but I have my whole life for fun."

She starts making a plan. She is going to call her mom. She is going to accept [the BA/MD program].

"Right now?" I ask.

Melissa nods and tells me decisions are due tomorrow. She picks up her phone, goes in the hall and comes right back. "Mom didn't answer."

She sits down at a computer and logs in. The [BA/MD program] website is down. She calls them. Someone helps her access the acceptance page on her iPad.

She picks up her phone again and looks over to me.

"When do you stop calling your mom before major decisions?" she asks me.

I laugh. "I don't know. I still call mine."

She calls her mom, who tells her she is making the right decision. She accepts. If all goes well, in 2021 she will be Dr. Chen.

The college decisions process contributed to many of the pressures of overachievement culture. Melissa believed that she needed to accept the most rigorous and prestigious college program available to her. This is the same student who took 15 AP exams. However, she was not certain that an accelerated BA/MD program was the healthiest choice for her. She also did not feel confident that she would be successful in such a program. By the time college decisions came out, Melissa had spent a school year working with our guidance staff, including me, on developing a self-care practice. During this difficult decision, she committed to waking up, coming to school, leaning on her connections, and exploring her feelings. Formerly, Melissa would have stayed in bed for days, wishing the decision would just go away. Instead, this time Melissa spoke at length with the student researchers, her family, and me about her potential options.

There was not a clear "right choice" for Melissa, or perhaps more accurately, there were multiple "right choices." Melissa is not the only academically high-achieving young woman I have worked with who made her college decision and then rescinded that choice within 48 hours to accept another offer. The stakes of this decision are high. In fact, in many cases, this is the most important decision a young person can make. As it was for Melissa, self-doubt is a compounding factor in a student's ability or inability to make a decision. Melissa's doubts stemmed from many places: She distrusted her ability to make the "right decision," she worried about her ability to do well in the accelerated and high-pressure medical program, and she was concerned about moving away from her mother and sisters. However, she ultimately decided to go for the higher stress, higher stakes option.

Self-Doubt's Continued Grip

Even after the student researchers were accepted to programs or higher education institutions, self-doubt continued to plague their decisions and planning. I asked Elaine how the college applications process impacted her self-concept. She shared,

> It made me feel like a nobody, to be honest. I felt average when applying for colleges and didn't feel like I've done anything special at all. For a while, I was sad because I didn't think I would get into [X University] and [would] disappoint my parents and family, but after I got in, I felt a lot better!

> I don't think my self-concept changed. I still feel like the same person. Maybe it fed my ego a little bit more. I don't know. It's great that I got in, but now I'm nervous about not flunking out.

Several of the student researchers, who were the highest achievers at Barnwood High School, honestly feared they would fail out of college. They had intense worries about not being able to complete their intended undergraduate degrees. They experienced feelings of imposter syndrome despite mounting evidence that they were capable and likely to succeed. During our study, the student researchers were accepted to highly selective colleges, graduated as valedictorians, and won generous scholarships. Yet, they told me they stayed up late worrying about failing out of college. In our work on self-care, we began to see the ways self-doubt impeded our mental health practices. We worked on reframing our self-talk and focusing on self-compassion and gratitude. Slowly, through our interrelated work on courage, connection, and self-care, we did find ways to alleviate self-doubt and promote confidence and care. Some of these actions that the student researchers took to promote self-care are discussed later in this chapter.

Confronting Self-Doubt

Naming and recognizing self-doubt helped us respond to our insecurities more directly, openly, and productively. We found that the more we talked about self-doubt, the more adept we become at recognizing and responding to it. Once the student researchers identified self-doubt, they could interrogate it, and determine whether it was well-founded or not. Then we could work together on a proactive path forward.

Near the end of our project, Leslie reconsidered her college applications and decisions process:

> With every *no* I received from colleges or scholarships, I felt worse and worse about myself. It seemed like their rejection was just validating all of my self-doubts. Of course, I knew that that wasn't the case, but for a while I took it really personally. I went over all of my accomplishments and thought "what more could I have done?" That was really unhealthy of me to do.

I asked her how she felt being on the other side of this precipice.

> Now that I am on the other side of the decisions process I know that I shouldn't have been so self-disparaging. That was a tough lesson for me to learn. It took a lot of tears for me to get over my rejections, but I did. And I think I am stronger for having gone through it.

Leslie was able to look back on her experiences in the college decision process with a growth mindset (Dweck, 2006). She recognized instances when self-doubt and criticism had led to "unhealthy" feelings. We both hoped that the next time she experienced self-doubt, she would be able to recognize and name it, and then dismiss it in a kind and gentle manner. Cultivating healthy and productive responses to doubt is an essential skill that will help students throughout their postsecondary lives; however, it is rarely addressed in school programs. Over time, we tried to refocus and retrain ourselves to see challenges and precipice experiences as opportunities to dismiss self-doubt and embrace self-care.

ALICE
An Abridged Case Study

Alice was a student from our first empowerment group, which we formed after hearing rumors of a self-harm pact associated with AP coursework. Before I took the gifted education position, I taught AP Language and Composition, and Alice was a student in my class. Like all of the teachers, I remember being shocked to hear about these mental health concerns among our brightest students.

Teachers loved working with Alice. Extremely polite, she sat in the front of the class and was an active, albeit quiet, participant. Alice's homework was always correct, complete, and turned in on time. She was a varsity cheerleader. She had top scores on her precollegiate standardized assessments and subtests. Everyone was impressed with Alice. When her name came up at a faculty meeting, one of my colleagues nudged me and said, "Talk about someone having their life together!"

Alice participated in the empowerment group, using the same strategies she did in my class. She had perfect attendance, showed up on time, completed all of the activities as assigned, and took neat notes on the readings. However, the more I paid attention, the more I saw that she wasn't particularly engaged with the content or interested in practicing vulnerability with our team. In fact, she told me later that she didn't see the point of some of these "softer" activities.

When Alice was at Barnwood, we would have both said that we had a close teacher-student relationship. Alice frequently studied in the gifted resource room, spoke to me about upcoming assignments, and asked for help with her college and scholarship applications. She even nominated me for a teaching award. However, I don't think we really got to know each other until a couple of years later when she was pursuing a double major at a prestigious college.

It was autumn of her sophomore year of college. I was hosting a health and wellness retreat for students in our sophomore AP program. Alice's younger brother was part of the group. When the event ended, his parents and Alice came to pick him up. It was the middle of the semester, and I was surprised to see her home from college. She gave me an enthusiastic hug and asked if she could stop by school to visit. I said, "Of course."

And thus began a series of regular visits and walks together. Alice told me she had "had an episode" at school and needed to take a semester off. Although she never went into details about the episode, we talked at length about her recovery and plans going forward. She was seeing a therapist, practicing fitness activities, and trying to figure things out. The consequences of this crisis were present in many of our conversations. One afternoon she told me,

> My parents have instilled a fear in me that I am going to have another episode and this time get kicked out of [college]. They're not scared that I'm not going to graduate or not going to get good grades. They're scared I'm going to get kicked out. So [laughs] now I have to worry about that too. . . . I worry that all my daydreaming is not going to happen at all. That I am being very unrealistic about what I am going to face when I go back and I won't be prepared despite all my therapy and all my personal motivation.

Alice made weekly appointments with me during my planning period. Sometimes she brought us coffees. We walked together on the trail behind school. During one of these walks, I noticed that she had stopped masking and now talked openly about her worries and triumphs. She told me about her friends and the many complications in her friend group. We talked about her goals; she was torn between medical school and graduate school in business. She talked about her family.

She also asked me about my coursework and where I thought I would be in 10 years. She asked if I struggled with perfectionism. I laughed. I had just finished a difficult mathematics course at the university that had shown me just how deep my personal perfectionism still ran.

Alice smiled and gave me the following advice, "My mom always says don't spend your time picking up the sesame seeds—wait, is that the right word? . . . yeah, picking up the sesame seeds. You should pick up your watermelons first. I'm not sure I translated that correctly." I asked if her mom told her this proverb in Mandarin.

She nodded. "It means to keep the big picture in mind."

I looked forward to our regular walks and enjoyed getting to know Alice as a college student. When the spring semester started, she went back to school and graduated on time with her peers. Once she returned to campus, I heard from her occasionally over text or e-mail. She even read a few draft chapters of my dissertation and joked that her notes were informed by a "great English teacher she had in high school." As I am working on this book, it has been more than a year since I have gotten one of her updates. I hope that she is doing well in graduate school and that she knows I am always only an e-mail away. I think sometimes people come into our lives at just the right moment. As teachers, it is our privilege to be there in those moments, to pay attention, ask questions, listen, and sometimes to suggest a long walk around campus.

Em*body*ing Self-Care

Each year, I invited Amy, my friend and colleague, to talk to our empowerment group. Amy has a background in biology, kinesiology, and nutrition. She would meet with our group during luncheons to present on the connection between brainpower and nutrition; however, every year the conversation quickly turned into a question-and-answer session about bodies. The students asked Amy questions about diet, menstruation, muscle building, and sexual health. Twice after one of her presentations, a student came forward and shared that she was struggling with an eating disorder that no one else had noticed.

Both times these confessions shook my confidence as an educator. I went home overwhelmed with guilt for not noticing sooner. How had I missed the signs (again)? Through our work on self-care, the student researchers taught me a difficult lesson—perhaps the reason we had missed the signs was because we weren't asking the right questions. Just as affective needs are seldom discussed in school, I realized that Amy's presentation was often the only time the students in our empowerment group had open conversations at schools about their bodies.

In my original research proposal for this project, I hadn't written anything about bodies. I mistakenly thought, "We'll just talk about health and wellness, you know, generally." The student researchers corrected me. They shook their heads and said, "We need to talk about bodies, our bodies, our relationship to these bodies, and our experiences with them."

Amy's presentation, although important, was insufficient to address the complex topic of bodies. Our research team helped me see that students' bodied experiences were more integrated into their lived experiences than I had considered. After all, bodies are central to students' identities as people, adolescents, and young women. Throughout our project, the students talked about their bodies more openly and frequently than I had anticipated. This required a dramatic shift in my own perspective about body talk with young women. As they did in so many ways, the student researchers helped shift my perspective about how we might better cultivate and nurture health and wellness in schools.

I had believed that the best way to support girls and young women in developing healthy body image was to not draw any attention to their bodies. In the gifted resource room I had a "survival drawer" in my teacher desk that I stocked with bandages, granola bars, and feminine supplies. I told my students that they could take what they need, without saying a word. The message was, "We do not have to talk about it." I believed that feminist teaching (and parenting) deemphasized bodies and appearances. I wanted the students in my program to know that who they were mattered more than how they looked. I worried that talking about bodies might undermine this key philosophy.

The students disagreed. They told me that their bodies were not always secondary and were rarely separate from their experiences. Yes, who students are will always be infinitely more important than how they look. However, our research revealed that how students feel about strength, courage, vulnerability, and confidence often manifests itself in their bodies. Further, it would have been impossible to engage in the work around self-care without also considering how these practices (e.g., nutrition, exercise, sleep, and mindfulness) manifested in our bodies. So we talked about bodies with candor, vulnerability, and frequent references to AP science courses, including biology, chemistry, and anatomy and physiology. There were several times when we called the women science teachers at Barnwood and asked them to join us in the gifted room and help us understand a body-related topic.

Physical Strength

Our research team planned team-building activities to help our group form trust and rapport. These activities strengthened our community, challenged us with an engaging low-stakes activity, and in several cases also provided cardiovascular benefits (e.g., taking fitness classes together). Throughout this research, we saw the importance of physical activity for self-care. Although the primary intention of our team-building activities was to have fun in a healthy low-stakes environment, we found that even in these activities it was sometimes difficult to let go of overachievement and perfectionism.

For one of our team-building activities, my friend Ericka, a personal trainer and bodybuilder, offered to teach us a kickboxing class. Her class, an hour of cardio and strength, left all of us (with the exception of Elaine) gasping for breath. We wore sweaty boxing gloves and punched and kicked heavy boxing bags until we could hardly move. After class we snapped a "survival photo" of our group. When we smiled for the gym manager, I noticed that Melissa was not looking well. She assured me she was fine. We went to the locker room afterward and Melissa headed straight for a trash can and started vomiting. Elaine got her water and told her she was going to be all right. Melissa told me that she had not done any "hard exercise" in a long time and wanted to see how hard she could run, jump, kick, and punch. She was testing herself, in much the same way she did when she took multiple AP courses. She wanted to push herself to her limits, or past her limits, even if doing so would result in physical consequences. Melissa believed that in this way she would discover what she was capable of. Practicing self-care with high-achieving and perfectionist young women is delicate. Melissa's experience at kickboxing is illustrative of the ways the student researchers sometimes found it challenging to let go of the need to compete, push, and achieve, even during our "fun" activities.

As a varsity athlete, Elaine also frequently spoke about wanting to push her body to its physical limits. Elaine's confidence, including her academic confidence, was linked to her capabilities and accomplishments as an athlete. As a smaller-framed powerlifter, Elaine often experienced injuries. When she was injured, she had to take a break from weight training for a week or more. The time away from her physical outlets was always challenging, and she told me she noticed a change in her overall mental wellness. She worried that the academic pressures in college might not be compatible with an exercise routine.

ELAINE'S JOURNAL
Senior in High School

June 2015

. . . Physically I always feel strong, not gunna lie. Unless I don't hit the weights I want to in strength training. Then I feel like I'm getting weaker, which is not good because I'm probably not getting weaker, just an off day. I don't think there's much else to say there. Well actually, maybe there is. Lifting-wise I'm pretty confident in my capabilities.

. . . I'm nervous I won't be able to work out in college because I'll be so busy with marching band and school. I don't want to get unhealthy. That would not be fun. Did you know that there was a study on how not exercising for a whole year affects a person who normally does so daily? They found that their brains literally shrunk, among other things declining, of course, such as balance, locomotor skills. Little worried . . .

During the course of our project, almost all of the student researchers discussed the connection they had experienced between fitness or physical strength and wellness or emotional strength. They spoke of running 5Ks, trying new fitness classes at the gym or recreation center, and camping trips.

Weight and Balance

The connection between being a "healthy weight" and feeling well was a conversation topic at several of our team meetings. Achieving, and even defining, "healthy weight" was variable and context-specific, depending on the student researchers' needs and backgrounds. For example, our groups included students who were underweight, overweight, and competitive athletes. All of these students had different needs when it came to weight goals and health. Although our dialogues about bodies became an important theme in our study, I was not interested in calculating any specific diet or weight-loss/weight-gain plans. Instead, I wanted us to explore the emotional connection between health and the body.

A few weeks into our project, Leslie shared,

> Obviously, there are the typical measures of physical health: BMI, weight, blood pressure, heart rate, etc. So I think those numbers should be within the normal range. I think you should exercise regularly and eat healthy. But, I also think it is important to be mentally and emotionally healthy. I think that means you should have people in your life who support you and who you can confide in. It means you should feel happy. You should be optimistic about your future. You should feel good in your own skin. You should feel confident. However, I think that most times all of these types of health are related.

Leslie frequently reflected on her self-care journey during our work on this research project:

> If you are physically healthy, you are more likely to be mentally and emotionally healthy. And that is a problem for me, because I am none of those things currently. So I just really want to start practicing more self-care because I think my emotional and mental health would improve as well.

Leslie and I talked at length about this. We brainstormed strategies to improve self-care. She reflected on the areas where she could improve her mental, physical, and emotional health. She made plans and then acted on those plans. In her own way, Leslie completed an entire research cycle around personal self-care, based in part on her relationship to her weight.

LESLIE'S JOURNAL
Recent High School Graduate

June 2015

I had to submit a physical to [Ivy League school], which meant stepping on a scale for the first time in a year. The results shocked me. I had gained 30 pounds my senior year. At first I was mortified. I started going through pictures and sure enough, though I hadn't noticed it at the time, I gradually gained weight across the entirety of my senior year. The worst picture was the one that my mom had bought of me in my cap and gown at graduation. It is sitting on our piano and serves as my inspiration to get more physically fit.

In the last 5 weeks I have lost 16 pounds. I am still far from my goal, but I know that I need to be proud of what I have accomplished so far. I know the journey will only become even harder when I start college, but I will try so hard to stay motivated. Right now something I am using to push myself is a future post I will make on my social media sites. I know it sounds silly, but I want to write a "Transformation Tuesday" post . . . about how I worked hard to get healthy again. So that is an end goal for me, but I tell myself that my immediate goal is if I lose one pound a week . . . that is a success—if I lose more, then that's even better, but I can't put unrealistic standards on myself. I need to lose the weight in a healthy manner that will promote keeping the weight off.

The high-stress nature of high-stakes school environments is often incompatible with self-care, particularly for high-achieving young women. Rather than focusing on her health, Leslie was managing multiple AP courses, safeguarding her "perfect" GPA so that she could earn valedictorian honors, and volunteering with multiple agencies. Although Leslie was upset by the weight gain at her physical, she thought back to the lessons from our research team and decided to engage in action instead of falling into a cycle of self-doubt and criticism.

Leslie called me a couple of days before she left for college. She asked if we could go on a trail walk together. We walked for several miles. She shared that the positive changes she made to bring more health and wellness into her life had inspired her parents and brother to do the same. All

116

four of them were practicing healthy eating and spending time walking and biking. She talked to me about her goals to keep up her self-care practice in college.

Managing Self-Care: Five Student Examples

During the years of this study, five student researchers stood out as consistently able to both navigate the challenges of high-stakes academic programs and maintain consistent self-care practices. Their peers often asked them how they did it, and as our project continued, I wondered the same. These students—Ana, Ty, Elaine, Rita, and Naomi—teach us important lessons about structures we can implement to support self-care at schools. Ana was the captain of the cross-country team and an avid volunteer in our local community. Every semester, Ty took on new hobbies; these ranged from weight lifting, to tutoring students with autism spectrum disorders, to teaching programming classes. Elaine was an all-state athlete, power lifter, and musician who regularly mentored younger students. Rita was a varsity athlete (she went on to play basketball at a Division I school) and was also very active in her church. Naomi was the editor-in-chief of our school newspaper; she also took advanced ballet classes and studied flute. All of these young women graduated at the top of their class and went on to attend their "dream" colleges.

They took the same advanced courses as the other student researchers, maintained the same "perfect" grades, yet managed to escape the extreme stress and panic attacks that so many of the other student researchers struggled with. This doesn't mean these five were better students or people; nor does it suggest that the others in our groups were constantly in states of high stress or panic. I mention these five because their emotional response to the high-stress academic programs at Barnwood might be able to offer us some insights into how schools can better safeguard wellness for high-achieving youth.

As a researcher, I looked for patterns in how these young women were able to have healthy and high-achieving school experiences (see Figure 5). On the surface, they had little in common beyond being high-achieving women. They had different identities, interests, and personalities. Some were introverted, and others were extroverted. They were different

Patterns Among High-Achieving High School Students With a Strong Sense of Self-Image and Self-Efficacy	
Courage	› They loved learning new skills. They consistently chose challenging tasks even when they weren't certain they would be successful. This included academic tasks, such as Calculus III (a university math course), and nonacademic tasks, such as learning a new sport. › They regularly pursued leadership and service work.
Connection	› They had diverse groups of friends and made time to nurture these relationships. › Although they frequented our gifted resource room, they had other safe places at school where they also went for connection, including the weight room, art room, journalism office, and their coaches' classrooms. › They had healthy relationships with their parents, whom they cited as their biggest supporters. (Interestingly, I knew some of the siblings of these five students, and not all of them had the same positive self-care experiences at school.)
Self-Care	› They practiced sports and fitness activities; three were varsity athletes, and two went on to play sports in college. In addition to organized sports, they regularly chose recreational fitness activities, such as hiking, pick-up basketball games, and Ultimate Frisbee for fun. › Although they worked hard on their advanced coursework, they managed to keep their competitiveness on the field and out of the classroom. › Although these students escaped the more extreme self-harm behaviors, they still experienced challenges and "little c" crises. They acknowledged that these were part of the human condition and were able to separate what was and wasn't within their sphere of influence. They problem solved these challenges proactively. › When they were working through something difficult, they had many people to go to for guidance and connection, including their families, peers, and teammates.

FIGURE 5. High-achieving students with a strong sense of self-image and self-efficacy.

races and ethnicities (Chinese, Mongolian, Vietnamese, and multiracial). They came from small (only child) and large (many children) households. Although they all had an aptitude for mathematics, they pursued many different academic passions. Despite these differences, each young woman had a positive self-image and healthy self-efficacy. Additionally, I noticed similar (although nuanced) patterns across courage, connection, and self-care.

When I think back to these five women's experiences at Barnwood, I am warmed by memories full of laughs and tremendous compassion for others. Ana, Ty, Elaine, Rita, and Naomi were among the students most likely to offer to help someone who was struggling with homework, to give a hug to a classmate who was having a hard day, and to stay after school and help me clean up the gifted room. They noticed these needs and jumped into action. Again, these five young women were not the only students who were eager to help, nor were they the only athletes, or the only ones who cited their families as their biggest supporters. In fact, without exception, all of the student researchers were kind, eager to help, and committed to justice. What differentiated these five was their ability to be present to the school environment in ways that sometimes let them notice needs before their peers did. I contribute this ability to their regular self-care practices that kept them away from perspective-clouding stress and panic.

Of all of the extraordinarily high-achieving young women I worked with at Barnwood, these five didn't need the empowerment group the same way the others did. Naturally, they benefited from being a part of the group; however, their safety nets and support systems were large enough that I think even without this school intervention, they would have been just fine.

These five young women didn't necessarily have easier lived experiences than their peers. In fact, they were more similar to the other student researchers then they were different. They experienced a full range of emotions, including sadness, joy, frustration, and contentment. We cried together, laughed together, and celebrated together. These young women had big worries for the world; they were especially concerned about injustice and violence. They also had more personal and deeply felt worries; they cried over sick friends and lost grandparents. They recognized that sadness and concern were valid emotions that needed to be felt.

Ana, Ty, Elaine, Rita, and Naomi remind us of the importance of diverse friend groups; meaningful school and extracurricular opportunities, including nonacademic outlets; and the self-perpetuating nature of self-care. They also teach us that although schools can (and should) set up better systems to promote self-care, there isn't a single or "perfect" algorithm that works for all students. For example, although ballet and journalism were important supports for Naomi, they likely would not have had the same effect on Rita. As teachers and administrators, we need to make sure that students are encouraged to participate in a range of extracurricular activities, including fitness/sports, and that they have plenty of opportunities to connect with peers whose lived experiences are different from theirs. Students need the autonomy to make some choices about what activities to pursue. Additionally we need to make sure all students have safe spaces at school to study, socialize, and visit with a trusted adult.

In Part III, I bring these lessons together to discuss the specific implications our project has for schools. I introduce the new framework for Wholehearted Teaching that emerged from this research, share how teachers can implement it in their schools, and close with insights on how we can take the lessons from this research "home."

PART III

Wholehearted Teaching

By the time this book comes out, my daughter Lilah will be 7 years old. Right now I tell people that she is 6 years old, and she corrects me: "Actually, Mama, I'm a little bit older. I am more like 6 ¾. You have to do the math."

I have been working on these research questions for her entire life. Several of the first student researchers took my AP English class while I was pregnant with Lilah. She has grown up around these questions, theories, books on gifted education, and more importantly, among the students whose stories are shared in these pages.

Lilah has played board games, read stories, and solved math problems with many of these brilliant young women. When she was 2 years old, she told Mia, one of the student researchers, that she wanted to be a pharmacist. Mia thought this was a perfectly reasonable goal for a toddler. However, she asked Lilah several questions to assess whether she was interested in pharmacy studies or pharmacology. When Lilah was 4 years old, Claudia, another student researcher, interviewed her for a radio story on women in STEM. Lilah told her about a storybook with a woman engineer character and offered Claudia her own working definition of feminism.

I would be remiss not to mention how being a mother to an exceptionally bright daughter has influenced my own interest in these research questions, as well as my urgency to find better affective supports for young women. In this final section of the book, I outline a framework for Wholehearted Teaching and give guidance on how to implement this framework in schools. Additionally, I explore how our personal communities affected the worldviews and perspectives each of us brought to this project. You will read about conversations I had with my husband, close friends, and colleagues around this research. Just as courage, connection, and self-care don't exist in isolation, neither do any of us. The themes in this study were interrelated and messy. And thank goodness—because it was in that messiness that we found wonderful connections, new friendships, and deeper learning than any of us could have imagined.

CHAPTER 6

A Framework For Wholehearted Teaching

Title

Hubris Lacks Perspective

Artist

Samantha Ding (2014),
senior in high school

Artist Notes

This piece shows how high school students sometimes lose perspective on their endeavors and problems. Teenagers are often described as thinking of themselves as "invincible" or extremely important. During the transition from high school to college and applying to colleges, students find this issue in the center of their world. We continually obsess over which colleges we got into, which colleges our friends got into, and what our future will be. However, we fail to get another perspective on this—the colleges we go to have only a limited impact on our futures. Just like the subject of this piece who is holding up a globe and thinks he is holding up the world, we sometimes need to readjust our perspectives.

Working on one research question often led us to a new and different question. These messy experiences are consistent with youth participatory action research methods. YPAR work engages the complex identities, personhood, and experiences of individuals in communities (Appadurai, 2006). This work is inherently complex. Although the students had diverse worldviews, cultures, contexts, and beliefs, they also shared several common experiences, pressures, and circumstances that stemmed from being high-achieving young women. For example, the stories the student researchers shared were often colored by pressure from advanced coursework, competitive applications (for college, scholarships, internships, and programs), and the quest to achieve top honors while coming of age as complex, bright, sensitive women (Hoy et al., 2006; Mathison & Ross, 2002; Rimm, 1999). This chapter introduces and situates the Wholehearted Teaching framework within the extant literature on gifted education and affective development.

The Wholehearted Teaching framework emerged from our research supporting high-achieving students in their schools and other communities. It is an extension and reimagining of Brené Brown's (2010, 2012, 2015) work on wholehearted living. Although the students learned from Brown's work, they shared that her research felt focused on professionals (or adults). They wanted a framework that applied specifically to students (young people). We knew that academic achievement needed to be a central tenant of any framework for schools, and particularly for one that would inform gifted and high-achieving programs. However, we wanted to look at achievement from a new affective perspective. To do so, we examined our own lived experiences, looking for spaces and practices that cultivated both affective and academic growth. Drawing on the courageous personal stories that the student researchers shared, as well as the conditions that made this powerful story sharing possible, I found new connections and interactions among our research themes. These connections and interactions ultimately led to this framework for supporting students in becoming courageous, connected, healthy, and high-achieving. I call this framework *Wholehearted Teaching.*

MY JOURNAL
Kathryn

October 2017

It was getting late, and I had hit a proverbial wall while working on this chapter. I was trying to think through the best way to illustrate the interactions between our different research themes. I had sketched out a series of coordinate planes, highlighted focus quadrants, and was trying to write an equation that would somehow *graph* to these spaces. It wasn't going well. Frustrated, I messaged Bel, a close friend who is also a gifted mathematician. She messaged me right back and asked how she could help. I sent her a Google Doc link with cryptic sketches and nonsensical equations.

She looked at the coordinate planes and asked me to name the axes. In literally a single breath (we'd switched to talking on the phone by this point), I told her about this project: "Okay, so courage is really the inter-action between vulnerability and strength. We usually get it wrong when we think about strength. We think about it as being about guardedness. And we create schools that are high-stakes, high-stress places where we expect students to achieve at high levels in environments that don't teach self-care."

"Uhum," she said as I raced on.

"And all of this has gendered implications, right? We expect kids to achieve in high-stress environments, we socialize them to think that strength is about guardedness, we don't teach self-care and then we are surprised when they experience social-emotional challenges. We're espe-cially surprised when we see this with high-achieving girls, because . . ." I paused for dramatic effect, "we all know that smart girls don't have problems."

Bel laughed empathetically at the familiar irony.

She looked over my notes again and said gently, "You know a coordi-nate plane doesn't actually work for what you are going for. If we use this model, we'd write an equation for a line, not an area."

I wasn't fazed. "Right. So, maybe what we need is an equation for a parabola. We'd need an inequality, right? To show the space under the line?"

"What if—" Because she is my friend, Bel resisted the opportunity to critique my late-night rudimentary (albeit creative) math ideas. Then, because she knows how distracted I get when I am excited, she double-checked to make sure I was listening. "What if we try something really simple before trying something really complex?"

She started drawing a Venn diagram. It turned out that I didn't need the support of a mathematician as much as I needed the support of a friend who intuitively understood the terms, conditions, and experiences of our study. She understood them because, so far, every high-achieving woman I've talked to about this work has said in her own words, "Yeah, that sounds like me." And so while the rest of my family slept, Bel and I mapped out a visual representation for the Wholehearted Teaching framework (see Figure 6).

Courage, connection, and self-care were the three central themes from our research. As I shared in Part II, these themes don't work in isolation. They are overlapping, dynamic, and interconnected. It is in this interconnected, dynamic overlap that we found spaces for new possibilities. The Wholehearted Teaching framework highlights these critical interactions between our themes, as well as the conditions needed to cultivate them in schools. These interactions include:

> Strength + Vulnerability = Courage
> Self-Care + High Achievement = Healthy Striving
> High Achievement + Vulnerability = Growth Mindset
> Self-Care + Strength = Wellness
> Connection × (Vulnerability + Strength + High Achievement + Self-Care) = Wholehearted Teaching

Although this framework is intended for schools, Wholehearted Teaching disrupts traditional or single-story (Adichie, 2009) notions of what it means to be a "teacher" or "student." Through our project, we discovered that teaching and learning are ubiquitous. Our own lived experiences, communities, and peer groups all served as critical teachers in our lives. In fact, as we examined our personal journeys, we found that there were times when we all served both as teachers and students. By taking a broader and more holistic view of learning, this framework offers guidance across the academic, social, and emotional landscapes of youth.

All of the feelings and behaviors on the Wholehearted Teaching framework exist on continuums. These continuums are fluid. I often observed

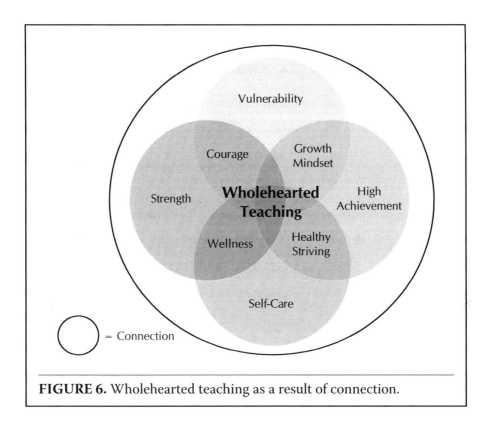

FIGURE 6. Wholehearted teaching as a result of connection.

students alternating between feeling strong and feeling limited, or feeling vulnerable and feeling guarded, during a single class period or even a single conversation. Wholehearted Teaching is the practice of helping young people (1) recognize these interactions and (2) recalibrate, when needed, back to courage, connection, and self-care. Counselors, teachers, and parents can use Wholehearted Teaching to consider different questions and practices to help cultivate healthy affective and academic growth for their students. Students can also use the framework as a personal reflective tool. The rest of this chapter describes and defines the key terms and interactions that make up Wholehearted Teaching.

Limited ↔ Strong

Strength is a layered concept that includes physical, emotional, and mental strength. We defined feeling strong as *independent interdependence* (Beauvoir, 1974; Gilligan, 1982; Young, 2005). Independent interdependence looks like taking academic, personal, professional, or creative risks in concert and cooperation with others. In her work on moral and psychological development, Gilligan (1982) asserted that interdependence refocuses our definitions of power to include the ways we care for and support others. By adding interdependence to our definition of strength, we intentionally disrupted the notion that strength is a solo activity. We consistently found that the students felt stronger when they were connected to stable communities, including classes, teams, families, religious groups, and peer groups. Community enhanced strength, whereas isolation limited it.

At the opposite end of the continuum from feeling strong is feeling limited (see Figure 7). Feeling limited translates to *isolated dependence*. This can look like being constrained or dependent on structures, on systems, or on people's approval or acceptance to the point that creative expression and risk-taking become nearly impossible. For student researchers, at the micro level, isolated dependence sometimes included pressures or expectations from parents, aspects of the hidden curriculum at school (such as which cultural groups took certain courses), microaggressions in extracurricular activities, and the exclusive culture of some social groups or cliques. At the macro level, these constraints included gender discrimination (Adichie, 2014; Collins, 2000; hooks, 2000), racism (Collins, 2000, Hartlep, 2013), and the hegemony of accountability in schools (Mathison & Ross, 2002). These pressures, rules, and social relationships all limited the students' ability to take creative risks, venture independent ideas, and forge interdependent (Gilligan, 1982) relationships.

What Does It Mean to Feel Strong?

The students' experiences as embodied people (described in Chapter 5) informed our understanding of physical strength. Feeling empowered, capable, and confident in one's body, on the field, the track, the stage, the court, and even in the classroom, was connected to our definition of physical strength. Within the context of our study, this understanding was also gendered. Young (2005) wrote that within a patriarchal society, "girls and women are not given the opportunity to use their full body capacities in free and open engagement with the world" (p. 43). The student researchers tended to fall into two groups: (1) student athletes who, although they experienced criticism and discrimination, generally saw themselves as physically strong, and (2) nonathletes who also experienced criticism and discrimination but often did not see themselves as physically strong. We had a wide range of student athletes in our program, some of whom participated in rec-

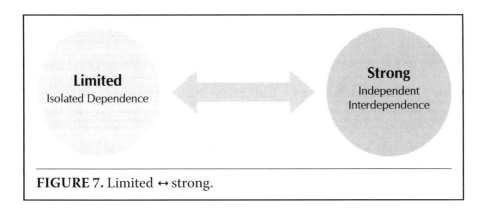

FIGURE 7. Limited ↔ strong.

reational and noncompetitive sports, and others who were varsity athletes in competitive school programs. In our empowerment groups we tried to create a space for these types of activities by going on hikes, practicing yoga, or taking kickboxing classes together.

Feeling strong included more than feeling physically capable. We were equally interested in understanding and developing mental and emotional strength. The student researchers characterized mental strength as feeling equipped for academic and intellectual challenges. As examples, the students wrote about debating high-level topics in their advanced classes, the thrill they experienced when they solved a complex problem, or the satisfaction of mastering a difficult piece of music. Mental strength is linked to academic perseverance, including working through an intellectual challenge, such as a complex math problem or difficult piece of music.

Emotional strength is the ability to respond to adversity with courage and confidence. Confidence doesn't preclude your voice from breaking, your knees from shaking, or your palms from sweating. The confidence we explored meant being willing to take a risk or do the "right" thing even when doing so was challenging. As examples, the students recounted experiences of speaking out against injustice, asking someone on a date, and admitting they needed help. Our research team found that emotional strength led to deeper connections and also to recognizing and experiencing a range of feelings more openly and fully (Young, 2005). Attending to feelings and emotions is congruent with both our project's feminist theoretical framework as well as our commitment to holistic affective education (Ferguson, 2006; Lorde, 1984; Lovecky, 2011; Rimm, 1999).

Guarded ↔ Vulnerable

Strength, as described in this book, is characterized by the capacity to make independent-interdependent decisions, including taking personal and academic risks. Because not all risks lead to success, vulnerability is compatible and necessary with this ideological pursuit. Brown (2015) wrote that vulnerability is "the willingness to show up and be seen with no guarantee of outcome" and that it "is the only path to more love, belonging and joy" (p. xvii). In our research, I defined vulnerability as the practice of taking personal and academic risks with uncertain outcomes. On the opposite side of the vulnerability continuum is guardedness (see Figure 8), which is characterized by limiting risk and making personal and academic choices based on the predictability of outcomes. As in the other theoretical continuums in this framework, there are times when we need both ends. There are times when it makes the most sense to "play it safe." However, playing it safe does not lead to new solutions, ideas, connections, or learning, and therefore should not be the educational status quo. Conversely, cultivating the conditions for strong vulnerability absolutely leads to deeper learning at all levels. However, cultivating strong vulnerability requires resocializing students and teachers to think differently about vulnerability and guardedness.

Students are socialized in many ways, particularly through media and sports, to connect strength with guardedness and to see it in opposition to vulnerability. Our project took a feminist stance to reconstruct and revalue vulnerability as a companion to strength. In her work on wholehearted living, Brown (2015) wrote about "the brave and broken-hearted rising strong" (p. 131). The idea of being broken, hurting, or imperfect (Brown, 2010, 2015) while also being strong and courageous, was a concept we explored throughout our project. Vulnerability is central to wholehearted living (Brown, 2010, 2012, 2015), humanizing research (Kinloch & San Pedro, 2014), and Wholehearted Teaching. Kinloch and San Pedro (2014) wrote that "discussing our vulnerabilities allowed us to engage in a dialogic spiral conversation in which we co-constructed knowledge" (p. 40). Being vulnerable is an intersectional act, meaning that multiple identities and circumstances affect the ease with which someone can be vulnerable while also being emotionally and physically safe. As educators, it is our job to make sure schools are safe places for healthy risk-taking, truth telling, and personal story sharing.

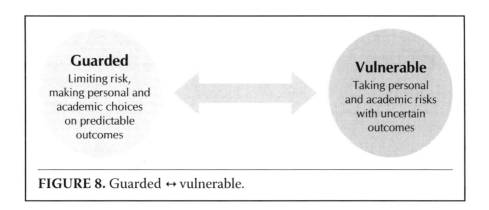

FIGURE 8. Guarded ↔ vulnerable.

Privilege, Power, and Vulnerable Stories

Privilege and power influence how personal stories are shared (or silenced). Within a hegemonic system, the common narrative is composed of dominant lived experiences (Gramsci, 2013). These stories perpetuate the status quo and are culturally low-risk to share. It is important to note that this doesn't make these stories less true or less valid. Wholehearted teachers affirm that all lived experiences are valid, including both those stories that align with the status quo and those that challenge it. Within our project, we shared many personal stories that complicated or responded to traditional perspectives on what it means to be a young woman or a high-achieving student. We explored multiple intersecting identities, including being a woman mathematician, an Asian athlete, and a Black gifted student. Telling these stories was an exercise in strong vulnerability. Practicing strong vulnerability requires emotional strength, disclosure, and embracing risk. Privilege is an important variable in assessing social, emotional, and sometimes even physical risk (Adichie, 2014; Belenky et al., 1997; hooks, 2000; Snyder, 2008).

Race, class, religion, gender expression, and sexual orientation were some of the identities that influenced risk in our story sharing. Marginalized groups typically have more at stake and receive less support for taking risks (Belenky et al., 1997; Collins, 2000; hooks, 2000). Additionally, the students shared that as teenagers they sometimes felt that their stories were less valued than those of their adult counterparts. An example of this is when our team was told that their radio stories needed to include adult interviews to grant them "expert credibility." The students' identities are intersectional, meaning they interact with each other. What it meant to be Asian was different for Elaine than it was for Melissa; likewise, what it meant to be Black was different for Rita than it was for Whitney. Many of our identities were fluid both in salience and identification. For example, Rita only some-times identified as Black. Although only one student researcher identified as low-income or poor, several of the student researchers had varied class experiences, including needing to pay their own way through college or having families who were willing and able to finance expensive college edu-cations. Even these markers were complex; for example, although Elaine's parents were able to pay for her college at a high-price institution, the mem-ory of their poverty in Vietnam is an important story in her family identity. Counterhegemonic storytelling meant complicating even common narra-tives about what it means to be a high-achieving young woman.

Strength + Vulnerability = Courage

Having safe spaces to voice truth is a precondition for healthy affec-tive development, activism, and autonomy (hooks, 1994). Phil Kaye (2012), a spoken word poet, referred to a "great vulnerability" as the ideological space where people connect through personal stories. Likewise, hooks's (1994) work on feminist teaching explored the need for safe spaces to voice lived experiences. Our radio stories, workshops, art show, and service proj-ects all are examples of strong vulnerability from our project. In Brown's (2012) terms, "vulnerability sounds like truth and feels like courage" (p. 37). In our project, we practiced vulnerability or rising strong (Brown, 2015) through courage, connection, and self-care, particularly in our personal story sharing.

The stories we tell ourselves about ourselves and the ways we trans-late those stories to others were critical to our team's work around cour-age (see Figure 9). Paying attention to our own self-talk informed many of our own vulnerabilities and growth areas for self-care. The students often first ventured courageous stories in the safety of the research community. Then, they shared their stories with larger audiences through our work with the radio stations and the special events we held. These stories offered stakeholders new, complex, and nuanced accounts of what it means to be a high-achieving young woman. For example, the student researchers invited the Barnwood administrative and guidance teams to their mental health art show in an effort to impact change in school policy and practice. In this way, our personal experiences became persuasive and political tools for making sense of the social-emotional landscape of school.

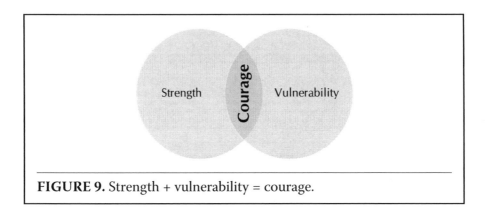

FIGURE 9. Strength + vulnerability = courage.

Low Achievement ↔ High Achievement

Our conversations about achievement walked a tenuous line between the academic status quo and a new range of possibilities. Certain types of academic achievement are constantly reinforced by the high-stress nature of the high school and college programs the students participated in (Hoy et al., 2006; Mathison & Ross, 2002; Robbins, 2006). In high schools and colleges, achievement is often measured by GPA and test scores. The student researchers were invested in keeping these quantitative measures as high as possible (Hoy et al., 2006). Consistent with the research on gender and achievement, the student researchers on this team were among the highest achievers at Barnwood, and in several cases, they were recognized as being among the highest achievers in the nation.

However, these quantitative indicators only tell part of a student's achievement story. Just as we reimagined other terms in our project, we aimed to reconstruct new, more holistic definitions of achievement. By attending to the interactions in the Wholehearted Teaching framework, I define high achievement as the use of courage and effort to work within or past one's potential, resulting in pride. Conversely, low achievement is being limited or stilted and unable to complete works within one's potential, resulting in insecurity or apathy (see Figure 10). Combining courage (healthy, vulnerable risk-taking) with effort (growth mindset, including a focus on process), while also attending to feelings and emotions (pride), can recenter school conversations about what achievement looks like and how we might cultivate deeper learning and growth. Teachers can engage in this conversation by asking their students questions about creative risks,

133

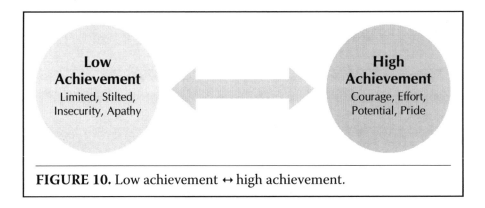

FIGURE 10. Low achievement ↔ high achievement.

dialoguing about process, and asking how students are feeling about their work.

If schools encouraged more multifaceted indicators of excellence (including music, the arts, athletics, and service), high-achieving students might feel less pressure to fit into only one narrow, measurable definition of school success. Broadening our understanding of success and achievement could lessen the likelihood of a masked affective crisis in schools. If teachers, educational leaders, and college committees shifted the conversation about achievement to process, potential, and pride, we might see more creative solutions, complex problem solving, interdisciplinary connections, and courageous students.

Self-Harm ↔ Self-Care

Self-care is an intentional decision to practice behaviors that relieve and balance physical, emotional, and mental stress. Self-care practices can be context- and identity-specific. For example, sometimes self-care looks like cuddling up with a good book, and other times self-care looks like going dancing with friends. Wholehearted Teaching gives a framework to consider, name, and act on current feelings and needs within a given situation. Some of the ways we encouraged self-care in our empowerment group included deep breathing, laughing, getting enough sleep, connecting with a positive peer group, practicing gratitude, healthy eating, fitness, celebrating successes, relaxation, and rest.

By contrast, self-harm is characterized by unhealthy behaviors that exacerbate physical, emotional, or mental stress (see Figure 11). Self-harm behaviors can also be context- and identity-specific. For example, some-

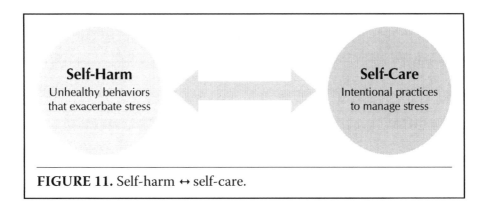

FIGURE 11. Self-harm ↔ self-care.

times a student knows she would feel better if she talked about a situation with her mom or if she stopped studying AP Biology at midnight and got a full 7 hours of sleep. Even though she knows this, the pressures she feels in other areas or insecurities she has about acceptance or achievement cause her to keep the situation to herself or to study well past the point of exhaustion. Some of the self-harm behaviors we saw in our project included disordered eating, unhealthy relationships, not getting enough sleep, drug and alcohol use, cutting, suicide ideation, and others. Self-harm carries a particular connotation (e.g., cutting). During our project, I did see some extreme behaviors; however, more often the student researchers and I saw smaller daily choices that, although they exacerbated stress, were generally accepted as the norm in the high-achieving youth culture, such as chronically not getting enough sleep. Our hope is that self-care work can shift this unhealthy culture in schools.

The Wholehearted Teaching framework includes a wide range of behaviors that fall between the self-harm and self-care extremes. I observed students engaging in practices that managed their stress and then engaging in behaviors that exacerbated their stress, often within the same 24-hour period. Identifying these types of behaviors can help young people notice their actions and then more consistently choose healthy practices.

Self-care work is delicate with gifted and high-achieving young women (Brown, 2012; Rimm, 1999), particularly because of their perfectionism. Perfectionism toward self-care is counterproductive. In our student groups we saw behaviors and habits that started out as self-care (such as healthy eating or exercise) and then became so extreme that they no longer served the individual in a healthy way. Faith discussed how her battle with anorexia was an example of this. Wholehearted teachers need to guard against treating self-care as a competition. Instead we need to teach students the importance of recognizing when they are out of balance on the self-harm/self-care continuum and help them respond by recalibrating with grace and gentleness, and beginning again. It is helpful if teachers can model this practice themselves.

Self-Care + High Achievement = Healthy Striving

Healthy striving refers to valuing process as much as or more than product, seeking out opportunities for improvement and growth, and pursuing projects that are personally and intellectually fulfilling (Brown, 2012). Our visual arts project was one of our early explorations in this kind of healthy striving. In many ways, the masked affective crisis is a product of the interaction between self-harm and high achievement. By helping young people recalibrate to an ideological space that includes both self-care and high achievement (see Figure 12), the bright students in my programs were able to do amazing work and enjoy that work. Using healthy striving as a model concept, the student researchers ventured new ways to practice both self-care and achievement. In fact, we found that coupling self-care with achievement often led to more creative, innovative, and courageous projects and products.

Through our research, we tried to untangle the consequences of a hyper-focus on achievement (Kindlon, 2006; Robbins, 2006) and also disrupt status quo definitions of success. The students shared that the high-stakes and high-stress nature of school often led them to work in perfectionistic ways that compromised their self-care. Repeatedly, the students told me that they didn't see a way out of this cycle. Some of the skills they believed they needed to achieve at high levels in school were not the same skills they needed to lead happy lives.

Prior to our study and empowerment groups, the student researchers had not been encouraged in school to develop self-care, nor had they considered the ways self-care might work in concert with or even enhance achievement. When we introduced the students to self-care, healthy striving, and wellness, we saw huge spikes in happiness, satisfaction, pride, and achievement. Unfortunately, self-care and related topics are seldom part of the standard school curriculum. Adding affective education (Dabrowski, 1967, 1970; Ferguson, 2006; Gilligan, 1982; Gilligan et al., 1988; Lovecky, 2011; NAGC, 2014) to curricular and instructional planning in high school,

136

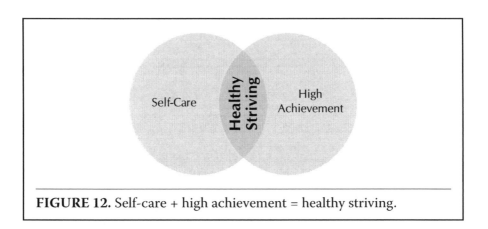

FIGURE 12. Self-care + high achievement = healthy striving.

college counseling, and gifted education programming is necessary to remediate the masked affective crisis and scale Wholehearted Teaching to the program, school, or district level.

Vulnerability + High Achievement = Growth Mindset

In the last 10 years, Carol Dweck's (2006) research on growth mindset has received considerable attention in schools. Growth mindset is characterized by the belief that it is always possible to learn new skills. Dweck showed that when students believe they can learn new things, overcome challenges, and see mistakes as part of the learning process, they achieve at higher levels. Brain research on neuroplasticity has shown that new experiences, challenges, and problem solving lead to new neural connections in the brain. These neural pathways in the synapses of the brain become stronger the more the brain is stretched and challenged.

For gifted and high-achieving learners this process can be complicated (1) by the ways teachers talk to high-achieving students and (2) by the curriculum available to these students. High-achieving and gifted students tend to receive numerous (and well-intentioned) messages from their teachers that celebrate successful exams, projects, labs, and products. The research (Dweck, 2006) shows that this kind of praise can be damaging to both achievement and mindset. When students hear that their summative product is perfect, they become nervous about maintaining that level of

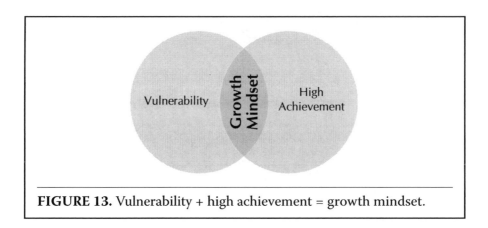

FIGURE 13. Vulnerability + high achievement = growth mindset.

perfection, which makes them less likely to take academic, creative, and personal risks, and can ultimately lead to lower achievement.

The availability of appropriately challenging curriculum for gifted and high-achieving students is context-specific. Access to advanced coursework varies according to school and district resources and priorities. Barnwood had extensive advanced course offerings, including abundant AP courses and connections with the local state university. However, I observed that even in this context, high-stakes and high-stress situations sometimes led our high-achieving students to "play it safe," such as not taking the more advanced math course or the extra world language course, or not opting for the more creative essay or science project idea. High-stakes environments tend to lead to risk-averse behaviors, meaning less creativity and innovation, and fewer of those new neural connections.

Art, music, service opportunities, and sports tended to be exceptions to this pattern. In all of these areas, the student researchers were consistently encouraged to take risks, make mistakes, and try new approaches. Although final products (games, meets, charity events, and concerts) mattered, much of the emphasis was on process. Coaches, teachers, and mentors in these areas seemed to know that focusing on processes led to more creative, effective, and impressive end results. One possible takeaway from this finding is to encourage more gifted and high-achieving students to get involved in art, music, service, and athletics. Another, more relevant takeaway is for teachers to learn from the best practices of these coaches, teachers, and mentors. These adults helped show students how vulnerability and achievement complemented rather than contradicted each other. For students who spent a lot of time in the art studio, in the music room, on the court, or on the field, I saw how these lessons translated to other school environments, such as choosing to take the more advanced course, write the more creative

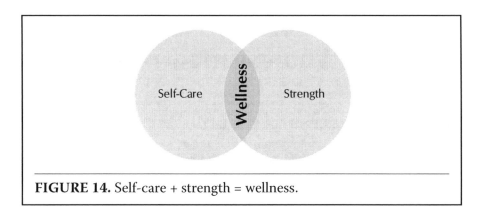

FIGURE 14. Self-care + strength = wellness.

essay, sign up for the extra world language they were interested in, or design the science project that no one else had tried yet. Wholehearted Teaching builds on the connection between vulnerability and achievement to nurture growth mindsets (see Figure 13), encourage healthy risk-taking, and ultimately cultivate new neural pathways of possibility.

Self-Care + Strength = Wellness

The World Health Organization (2018) defined wellness as "a state of complete physical, mental, and social well-being, and not merely the absence of disease or infirmity." Wellness is not only being free of illness (mental or physical) and pain (emotional or physical); it also means being able to enjoy life, to be fully present, and to thrive. These are ambitious goals in the context of high-stress and high-stakes schools. However, as our research has shown, the rewards of attending to student wellness include gains in affective and academic growth and development. Healthier and happier students are more successful socially, emotionally, and academically. In short, work around wellness is important. Although many of the interactions in the Wholehearted Teaching framework are related to wellness work, it may be helpful to understand wellness as the interaction between strength (physical, emotional, and mental) and self-care (intentional practices to manage and balance stressors; see Figure 14). As educators, we can foster wellness in schools by integrating a range of practices that foster feelings of confidence, courage, connection, and happiness. Conversations about feeling strong and practicing self-care should be part of the dialogue in all of our classrooms.

Connection: The Multiplier Across Wholehearted Teaching

The student researchers and I frequently came back to math to illustrate the ideas in our project. This could be because of our collective affinity for order, logic, and numbers. It might also have something to do with the way our teams processed information together. Regardless, as I worked on describing Wholehearted Teaching in a way congruent with our work, I found myself coming to back to equations, graphs, and algorithms. What follows is the equation I finally wrote to describe this new teaching framework as well as the multiplying impact that connection has across all of our Wholehearted Teaching variables.

$$C \times (V + S + HA + SC) = WT$$

C = Connection   HA = High Achievement

V = Vulnerability   SC = Self-Care

S = Strength   WT = Wholehearted Teaching

See Figure 6 (p. 127) for a visual representation of this equation. As both the equation and the visual representation illustrate, connection initiated and enhanced every theme in our study. The lessons we learned about connection may be the most significant social-emotional takeaway from our research project. Students, like all human beings, need groups they belong to, people they trust, and communities that accept them for who they are and affirm their stories by saying—although often in slightly different words—"I see you and recognize that your experiences are valid." Although our research team was investigating the question of how to improve affective supports in the stressful high school and college contexts, it turned out our research community was also the answer.

As a participatory researcher, I knew that the connections our research group formed would be important. However, I had not anticipated that the students would overwhelmingly cite the friendships they made and the lessons they learned about the importance of peer groups as the most significant product of our work. As Leslie boarded her plane for college, she sent the following text to our group:

Leslie: I'm thinking of you this morning. I'm about to board my plane to [X city], and I'd just like to wish you all the best of luck! You're going to be so successful, and I'm glad I can call you my friends. :)

Leslie's short text speaks to the evolution of our community. I believe the potential we found in creating supportive community groups can be replicated in high schools, undergraduate programs, and community organizations. Through questioning, dialoguing, and sharing our personal experiences (Belenky et al., 1997; Hesse-Biber, 2012; Reinharz, 1992), we made sense of the nature of high-stakes and high-stress schools, issues of identity, and support practices needed to help students find healthy pathways where they could experience success. The positive impact of belonging to a collaborative team of women, who shared openly and honestly and wanted to contribute to social change, was profound (hooks, 2000).

MY JOURNAL
Kathryn

January 2018

The community we built as a research team was vital; however, each of us working on this project also belonged to other communities where we shared our work. For example, Elaine talked about these themes with her track mates, Melissa with her mom, and Leslie with her new peers in college. We invited our friends to special events and luncheons. The people in each of our personal communities heard about our lessons, attended team events, shared our celebrations, and helped us problem solve some of our challenges. This is true for me, too.

One afternoon, Chris, my husband, was reviewing a few of the chapters of this manuscript. He's gotten to know several of the students from attending our research events and presentations, visiting with them when they dropped by the house, or seeing them in the community. In fact, just earlier that day we had run into one of the students at a local bakery.

Chris has told me that some of the sections are harder for him to read. While reviewing one of these sections, he put his laptop down and asked,

"What do you think what was the most important lesson these students learned?"

I considered his question for a few minutes and responded: "Learning that they were not alone. Before this project, so many of the students thought they were the only one who struggled with anxiety, depression, stress, loneliness, or imposter syndrome. Finding out that, actually, these are shared experiences and that there are tools we can use to work through them was pretty amazing. Recognizing that they weren't alone in these experiences taught them that maybe there are actions we could take to bring about change. This really fueled our work around wholeheartedness."

While Chris and I were visiting about my research, our son was reading a book to our daughter. Chris watched our children for a few minutes, considering, and then turned back to me and said, "I hope lots of teachers read this and realize what a difference they can make."

Through our commitments to monitor patterns of participation, mitigate power dynamics (Appadurai, 2006; Tuck, 2009), affirm, and listen (Adichie, 2009; Hesse-Biber, 2012; hooks, 2000; Reinharz, 1992), we became a vibrant educational community. We worked on the personal, interpersonal, and public spheres, in that order (hooks, 2000). Through examining our own self-concepts, through supportive and personal story sharing, and through taking action on issues that mattered to our team, we saw dramatic increases in our personal and collective self-confidence, self-efficacy, and self-image. Every student researcher commented on the ways connecting to this group influenced them personally. As a teacher, I also saw the ways these practices deepened the culture of my classroom.

A Multiplicity of "Right" Answers

Our academic identities (Lovecky, 2011; Kerr, 1994; Rimm, 1999) and socialization as high-achieving women (Maurer, 2011; Robbins, 2006) caused us to approach this project with a pointed intentionality to find the right answer or solution. We had three central research questions, and each of us, in our own ways, wanted the algorithm to solve for x. However, instead of a right answer, we found points of contention, blurred lines, and fuzzy definitions. We had to learn that this didn't mean we had failed to solve the research problem. In fact, this unlearning was an important outcome of our project (St. Pierre, 2000). We used feminist epistemologies (particularly, Adichie, 2015; Anderson, 1995; Belenky et al., 1997; Belsey, 2002; Collins, 2000; hooks, 2000; Snyder, 2008) and YPAR methodologies (Heron & Reason, 2001; McIntyre, 2008; Morrell, 2004; Taylor et al., 2006) to unlearn the positivist drive of pinpointing a solitary answer. In this unknowing, we found richer and more complex answers (yes, multiple answers) to our questions. We learned that in our own lives, there often is not a right answer; rather, there are infinite right answers. This multiplicity informed the lessons we offered to support practice, theory, and research for high-achieving and gifted young women.

We started our project with big questions about lived experiences and social-emotional needs. We thought, in turn, that we would discover big trends. We were looking for (capital T) Truths about gifted young women, identity, and school. We were surprised when, instead, our findings almost always surfaced in the form of personal truths. The more we learned about ourselves, our experiences, and our stories, the more progress we made on pushing knowledge and action forward with this project.

A few weeks after Leslie joined our research group, she shared that she hoped our project would help her with

> some self-discovery (which I know is already happening, as writing journals is allowing me to think about myself in a metacognitive way). I think I also want to develop some better habits before I go away to college. And by habits, I mean that I want to develop a better self-esteem and self-image, because those are things I lack. I'd also like to explore why I believe some of the things I do (like why I have such a low self-esteem).

When we closed the project, I asked Leslie if she thought she had met these goals. She answered immediately, "Yes! I'm not cured. It's still a process, but I am in a much healthier place now than when we started this." The personal growth that Leslie spoke of informs those bigger lessons that teachers and schools need to create new conditions to support Wholehearted Teaching practices. Because of her experiences in our group, Leslie left the project stronger, more confident, and healthier (all her terms). As both a teacher and facilitator of this project, I call that a success.

Our research attempted to fill an important gap in educational practice and literature. We wanted strategies to bolster affective supports for
high-achieving young women. My hope was that if we created these conditions in high school, students would then take this skill set with them
to college. This book offers longitudinal data that both affirms and com-
plicates this hope. As with every other finding in this study, I learned the
answer wasn't that simple. Absolutely, the strategies students learned in our
empowerment groups helped them as they tackled social, emotional, and
academic challenges in college. Consistent with our research findings, we
saw that challenge was both inevitable and often an opportunity for growth.
When those challenges came—as of course, they did—there were times
when the students were able to recalibrate to courage, connection, and self-
care and find their way beyond the challenges. There were other times when
this wasn't enough. Often in these cases, elements of the challenges were
beyond students' sphere of influence. In these instances, we sometimes saw
the need for additional interventions, including medical leaves, treatment
centers, additional counseling, or taking a completely new course of action.
Needing additional support doesn't negate Wholehearted Teaching as an
effective support for these students. In fact, being open to more support is
consistent with a wholehearted approach. The students tell me that even in
these extreme cases, they found themselves thinking back to our luncheons,
classroom conversations, and group activities. Students remembered our
lessons on courage, connection, and self-care, and in these lessons they
found (and continue to find) practical strategies they can use to identify
healthy pathways and the knowledge that they are not alone. The next chapter outlines how educators can implement the Wholehearted Teaching
framework in their schools.

CHAPTER 7

Implementing Wholehearted Teaching

Title

Courage: A Cyclical Journey

Artist

Decrito Tivnan-Oda (2017), high school teacher

Artist Notes

Life is a cycle, and living it in courage makes us embrace the fact that in every difficulty we encounter and in every struggle we undergo within this difficulty, there is always a break of dawn that guides us toward the rays of hope of the sun. With love, openness, and joy, we can bask in this cycle of life. After all, there are many bright colors around to appreciate!

I've been asked by several teachers for "clear, step-by-step directions" on how they can implement Wholehearted Teaching in their schools. This request always makes me smile; it reminds me of my students. Just as the student researchers wanted to proverbially solve for x, my teaching colleagues essentially asked for a Wholehearted Teaching algorithm. I suppose everybody likes an answer they can measure.

In this chapter, I'll share the conditions that made this work possible and some of the strategies I used to support those conditions at Barnwood. I present this information with the caveat that replicating this project is contextualized by the students, teachers, schools, and communities you are working with. Much of this work centers on themes that are messy and can't be quantified. Every time I ran an empowerment group and every time we orchestrated a YPAR project, there were unique challenges and celebrations that shifted the ways Wholehearted Teaching worked in our communities. That said, there were some common commitments that ran across all of these projects. This chapter is shaped around those commitments, which are outlined in Figure 15.

Practice Courage, Connection, and Self-Care

In the summer of 2017, I led a professional development series for teachers of high-achieving youth. This was the first time I attempted to operationalize how teachers might implement Wholehearted Teaching in their classrooms. I had met with this group of educators 6 months beforehand and knew they were interested in exploring the role of courage in schools. Using many of the aspects of the Wholehearted Teaching framework, we set out to explore what it means to teach and lead for courage. It turned out that before we could begin our professional exploration, we had to engage in some personal work. We shared our central stories. Some of the topics were the same as those in the student groups, including self-doubt, gender and leadership, identity, and even the complicated relationships we still have with our mothers. Some of them included more adult topics, such as divorce and parenting. We studied scholarship around courage and vulnerability. We engaged in team-building activities, including eating together and going out dancing. We laughed. We cried. We processed in person and over text. Our series culminated in a community showcase on teaching and

Implementing Wholehearted Teaching: Nine Common Commitments
Practice courage, connection, and self-care. Implement the Wholehearted Teaching framework in your own life before (and while) nurturing these themes in schools.
Be an active listener. Young people need to be heard, affirmed, and valued. Have a system in place to make sure you are listening more often and more actively to students. Active listening only happens with intention.
Encourage student leadership. Young people need authentic opportunities to be researchers, presenters, problem solvers, and agents of change. Say yes to student-led initiatives.
Increase opportunities for play and laughter. Don't make play novel or auxiliary to your school day; build it into your regular class experiences.
Leverage community expertise. Reach out to teachers, counselors, administrators, parents, and community professionals for help in facilitating regular conversations about courage, connection, and self-care.
Schedule peer-group meetings. Create peer groups and gatherings where young people can regularly explore topics and activities not associated with schoolwork or academics; do not assume these groups are happening organically.
Integrate self-care into your classroom environment. Incorporate self-care into your teaching and lesson planning. Use it both as a topic for discussion and as a condition to cultivate.
Make storytelling part of your school community. Personal storytelling has the potential to help students make sense of their lived experiences, to build bridges between people, and to heal. Give students space to share personal stories.
Honor nuance. Each student group, each class, and each school will operationalize all of these concepts differently. Take the lead from your students.

FIGURE 15. Common commitments of Wholehearted Teaching.

living for courage. We invited our colleagues, friends, and members of the College of Education to join us. Everyone was astounded by the stories that were shared and the power of those stories to bring us closer together.

Wholehearted Teaching encompasses themes that are not exclusive to the needs of gifted and high-achieving young women. Courage, connection, and self-care are universally important. In my work with teacher groups around these themes, I've found that (1) professionals also don't have enough opportunities to explore these ideas and (2) when given the opportunity, educators find this work both challenging and important. I've learned that when I introduce Wholehearted Teaching to groups of teachers as a tool for student support, we have to explore the themes personally before we can explore the framework professionally. In order for teachers to be role models and facilitators in a praxis-based dialogue around courage, connection, and self-care, we need to be familiar with and wrestling with these concepts ourselves. Facilitating work around courage, connection, and self-care does not mean you practice these concepts perfectly. In fact, students can often learn more from hearing about how teachers make mistakes, encounter challenges, respond to adversity, and still persist even when doing so is hard. Opening up honest dialogues about the ways we are all in progress is part of the narrative that undergirds Wholehearted Teaching.

Be an Active Listener

Active listening will not happen by accident; it requires intentionality. Through this project, I learned both the importance of active listening and the challenges inherent in practicing it in schools. Schools are full of distraction. Teachers are constantly pulled in a million different directions; our attention is diverted, and it seems as though everyone is in a hurry. Therefore, practicing active listening requires both creativity and advanced planning around space and time.

MY JOURNAL
Kathryn

Spring 2015

On One-on-One Dialogues

This week we carved out extra time for extended one-on-one dialogues. . . . These dialogues reminded me how important it is to set aside one-on-one time in all relationships. The student researchers and I were already close, but sitting together and listening, truly listening, was striking. During finals week, quiet space is a scarce commodity at our school, so we had to find creative spaces to talk. We visited in Claudia's car, the guidance conference room, a supervisor's large office, and the small annex next to the gifted center. Each of the interviews lasted about an hour.

. . . I noticed the students' voices: each varied and distinct but also similar in their youth and hope. They were confident and questioning, emotional, warm, full, and edged with humor. I noticed new qualities in their voices. Claudia's voice reminded me both of my sister and my close friend Lisa. I noticed the softness in Jessica's voice, the warmth in Faith's voice, the reflection in Leslie's, and the clarity in Elaine's. These were emotional conversations for all us. Eyes filled with tears. Voices cracked. For a few of the students this was the longest uninterrupted time I had spent listening to them. True listening is a gift, and it is one that is hard to give in the high-stress culture of school.

At Barnwood, we had a special place set aside for active listening. If a student said she needed to meet with me in this office, I knew that meant she needed my full attention. We didn't bring our phones, homework, or grading into the space. Because everyone in the gifted program knew this room was set aside for listening, students didn't interrupt with questions about calculus, verb conjugation, or when the cafeteria would next be serving cheese sticks. Students also knew that I was most easily available for these conversations before school and during lunch breaks. Setting structures around time and place facilitated more active listening. Students and I also practiced a lot of walking dialogues. We were often seen walking around campus, talking through a situation, experience, or challenge. Sometimes the act of moving and not having to look someone right in the eye facilitated more dialogue and processing. I learned two vitally important lessons from active listening to students: (1) active listening is the heart of all relationships and (2) educators need to think differently about crisis.

Prior to this research, I had conceptualized personal crises as those major challenges I encountered when I first took the position in gifted education. However, the student researchers taught me to view crisis more complexly. Yes, the major moments of depression, disorder, loss, and abuse are absolutely (big C) Crises. However, crisis, like many of the concepts in our study, exists on a continuum. Less extreme (little c) crisis experiences, such as arguing with a best friend or mother, an injury before a big athletic event, not getting a scholarship, needing an outpatient medical procedure, or a parent losing his job, were also crisis moments experienced by members of our research team during the course of our project. These experiences were important in understanding and addressing the social-emotional needs of our student groups.

Recognizing and validating the crises of the young women I worked with was essential in helping them to process and work through the challenge. Although each crisis experience and each individual is unique, we found that courage, connection, and self-care were effective strategies across crisis experiences. Unfortunately, this skill set is seldom taught in schools or teacher preparation programs. Instead, standardization, accountability, and academic emphasis tend to dictate curriculum and instruction in high-stakes, high-stress school contexts (Mathison & Ross, 2002; Robbins, 2006).

Encourage Student Leadership

Wholehearted Teaching hinges on students being given permission and encouragement to make decisions that matter. Having agency to identify and work on issues that are important—to take risks, make mistakes, implement new projects, and practice leadership—was essential to the way students learned and thought of themselves as learners. How much permission and encouragement do we give students to take these kinds of risks? How often do we honor students as decision makers in schools? These are essential reflective questions for implementing Wholehearted Teaching. Two of the vehicles we used to highlight and cultivate agency and student leadership were youth participatory action research (YPAR) and service learning.

Students as Researchers

YPAR is centered on understanding community issues in order take action and find solutions (Heron & Reason, 2001; McIntyre, 2008; Taylor et al., 2006). For more specific information about YPAR, see the Methodology Appendix. Asking students to identify issues that matter to them, problems they want to solve, and challenges they are having, and then affirming that students are important leaders in finding the solutions, validates both student leadership and potential. Although referred to by different names, the social-emotional needs of gifted young women were deeply personal to everyone involved in this research. And so, the masked affective crisis was a problem we set out to solve.

We could all point to evidence of the masked affective crisis in our own lived experiences. Throughout our study, we continued to see evidence of this crisis in our communities. Two of the student alumni from our empowerment groups took medical leaves from their selective colleges for mental health. Thankfully, they were both able to return to school before the study closed. During our project, we lost one alumna to suicide. These women were all in gifted programs throughout school, all were high achievers in their academic endeavors, and all were well-liked by faculty and peers. In many ways, this book is a call to pay more attention to the students hiding in plain sight on your school honor rolls.

Throughout our project we saw countless examples of divergent thinking ability, excitability, sensitivity, perceptiveness, and entelechy (Dabrowski, 1967, 1970; Dabrowski & Piechowski, 1977; Lovecky, 2011). This intensity was often complicated by anxiety and the desire to appear "normal," even when the students didn't know exactly what "normal" might mean. Reshaping the conversation to one in which students were told they had agency to develop solutions, respond to systems that were not working for them, and present as experts on their own lived experiences gave us new knowledge about the affective crisis and also helped us remediate it.

Service Learning

We all need more opportunities to meet people who are different from us, to forge new friendships, and to engage in meaningful community-based work, not because it looks good on college applications but because it makes us better human beings. Like YPAR work, service-learning projects are cyclical and fueled by agency and reflection.

The student researchers were all involved in a schoolwide initiative at Barnwood to increase service in our school and broader community. This initiative was student-led; projects and organizations were selected and implemented by young people. Asking students what issues they see in their communities and how they might make a difference or impact change is consistent with the strength and connection threads of the Wholehearted Teaching framework.

Service learning is a powerful bridge between the affective and cognitive domains. Successful service-learning projects change the landscape of the classroom by including the community and community-based organizations as learning spaces. Further, service learning can humanize wisdom. Students learn from the elderly, from people with disabilities, from children living in poverty, from medically fragile communities, from refugees, and from support staff in their own schools. In my teaching practice, I saw how these relationships were important in perspective-setting and democratizing knowledge. Through community-based partnerships, our students were able to make a tremendous impact. They didn't have to wait until they were adults or professionals to make a difference, which is a powerful personal lesson for both educators and students to learn. Our students raised funds to subsidize the cost of summer programs for youth in poverty, they cleaned up our local community, they forged new friendships with students receiving special education services, they sewed blankets for children in foster care, they planned events at a nearby retirement community, and they launched educational campaigns around cancer research and gender inequality. Wholehearted Teaching reminds us not to underestimate the dynamic potential of student leadership.

Increase Opportunities for Play and Laughter

Too often the importance of play is missing from secondary school curricula, particularly in our advanced courses. As I attempted to integrate play into my gifted classroom, I operated under four guiding assumptions:

1. Student happiness matters.
2. Laughing is linked to social-emotional well-being.
3. Laughing and play lead to positive classroom culture.
4. Play and learning are not mutually exclusive endeavors.

I encouraged students to gather in our classroom for lunch and stocked the room with board games and puzzles. Lunch shifts in the gifted resource room at Barnwood were a flurry of hamburgers, chicken nuggets, crosswords from *The New York Times*, marching drill cards, strategy games, playing cards, and programming problems. Creating a space for young people to play games, laugh, eat, problem solve, and feel safe may be one of the most important structures I set up at Barnwood.

One year, I was assigned a challenging last block advisory period. This particular group had endless energy, boundless extroversion, and a gift for distraction. In those first few weeks, I left that class exhausted, but this all changed one day in mid-September when my advisory students were making paper airplanes. I raised my left eyebrow and decided to take a risk. I told the class that if we studied for the next 60 minutes, then we would have a flight contest. Surprised, students took out their textbooks and studied. An hour later airplane construction began. Our fly-off was epic, and the winning model contradicted everything we thought we knew about aerodynamics.

I continued to use play as a teaching practice with this advisory. In October, we started a running club. One of my students, who had never participated in organized track and field, ran a 5-minute mile right off the bat. He went on to run varsity track and cross country for Barnwood and later earned a college running scholarship. Over the next couple months, one of my most challenging advisory classes became one of our most successful academic and affective communities.

However, not all of my gifted students were jumping up and down to participate in these play-based moments. Often the highest-achieving students were the least likely to close their AP textbooks and compete in a paper airplane fly-off or run races around the lake just south of campus. With these students, I talked candidly about the link between laughing and health. I also told them that sometimes these activities were not optional. They already had full academic lives; often these students were missing time to laugh with likeminded peers. We brought these elements to our group meetings and explained why we were doing so. We modeled that it is important to take time to go for a run, to dance, to stretch, to watch silly movies, and to bake chocolate chip cookies. When the student researchers went to college, they told me they were grateful for these lessons and were still scheduling time for them.

Implementing Wholehearted Teaching requires teachers to identify places where they can schedule in play and laughter and also to look for moments when a laughter break is essential. For example, one day a group of sophomore students stopped by the gifted resource room after finishing 5 hours of standardized testing. I looked at their tired faces and thought, *These students need recess*. We walked over to a nearby playground. We raced and jumped and swung on the swings. We acted like first graders. We laughed a lot. One of the students told me, "I thought this was going to be the worst day of the year, but you made it the best."

Leverage Community Expertise

Wholehearted Teaching does not exist in a vacuum. During this project we frequently brought in experts from our community to help facilitate conversations about courage, connection, and self-care. Wholehearted

Teaching is most effective when thought of as a community project rather than only a school-based intervention. I leaned on the wisdom of my teacher colleagues, counselors, administrators, support staff, and friends. I invited guests to our team meetings. I brought students to new places in our community, including the university's women's center, the gym where I take fitness classes, community parks and trails, and our NPR member station. Likewise, the student researchers also leaned on and involved the expertise of their personal communities.

For example, the day that our radio stories aired, Faith used social media (Facebook and Instagram) to share her story with a broader audience. Her Instagram account is publicly viewable. Her Facebook account is visible to more than 1,500 contacts. She posted the following text (and the two mentioned photos) to both of these social media accounts. She wanted to use her story to bring greater awareness to the issues that were personally important to her. In her post she shared her personal struggle with her friends, classmates, teachers, pastors, and relatives.

FAITH'S SOCIAL MEDIA POST

June 2015

This is the best kind of Transformation Tuesday. In the left photo I was 99 pounds, depressed, and quickly starving to death. In the right photo I'm healthy and on my way to accepting and being happy with who I am and the body God gave me. It's been a LONG (and still continuing) battle and I'm posting about this today because today my radio story about eating disorders and their misconceptions/stigma aired on [local NPR affiliate].

There's a stigma that if you're struggling (especially with mental health issues) it's your own fault, and that is simply NOT true. We don't always get to choose our battles. If there's one thing I learned from this and want to share, it's that EVERYONE is fighting something under the surface that you probably know nothing about. The best thing to do is to assume nothing, but instead listen, love, and treat everyone with the kindness and open mind they deserve. You never know how far a kind word or a hug will save someone or how much a quick judgement and false assumptions can hurt.

Faith's post garnered a large response. More than 220 people "liked" the post, and 34 people commented on her Facebook account. Faith responded to each comment. The Instagram post resulted in another 35 comments and 169 "likes." That is an engagement of more than 400 people in Faith's networks, all of whom were talking about mental health and eating disorders because of her personal vulnerability and courage. We saw an increase in agency as a result of our work, and I credit this increase specifically to our lessons around courage.

The comments were all supportive. In fact, I saw a ripple effect in many of these notes. Faith's courage in sharing her personal social-emotional challenges, including struggling with depression and anxiety, led to others opening up (in some cases, for the first time) about their own struggles with mental health. In this way, Faith's personal experience and act of courage directly contributed to an unmasking of the affective crisis. For example, one person wrote,

> Thank you for sharing this. . . . As you may know, I have my own struggles with mental illness. I hope your path to the future is positive and that you continue to go forward. I'm glad you are recovering.

Another person wrote, "Thanks for being open and sharing. May your sharing and words of wisdom be helpful to others. Love and prayers!"
Still another wrote,

> Very well said. You are helping so many people that you will never meet because of your strength and honesty in sharing your story. And for fighting the stigma. I opened my "closet" when I did a Lenten sharing at church years ago and talked about my lifelong struggle with depression. Prayers and love for you and your terrific future!

The student researchers learned that their voice and their stories had power to impact change at the hyperlocal level (within their own peer groups), in their school communities, and even in broader city and state dialogues. The students told me that as they connected to other people through courageous storytelling, they often noticed they were more hopeful about human nature, including their own ability to heal.

Schedule Peer-Group Meetings

I am often asked how I set up empowerment groups at Barnwood. Although each school context will be different, it can be helpful to study an example. Here is what we did. At the beginning of each school year, I partnered with our advanced teachers and counselors to identify the highest-achieving young women in the junior class. I then sent invitations to each of these young women explaining our empowerment group objectives and schedules. The vast majority of students we invited participated in the program. Our formal group meetings ranged from 12–20 students in attendance. We had these formal meetings once or twice a month, usually over lunch potlucks. These meetings were organized around a focus topic, such as self-care, healthy relationships, nutrition, and communication.

Additionally, we had numerous informal group meetings. Each year, soon after the group started, the students began meeting for lunch in my classroom every day. This happened every year without any additional organizing on my part. These daily lunches led to a continuous conversation about achievement, self-care, and community. It also made our formal meetings touchpoints in a larger dialogue, as opposed to separate or stand-alone events. During 3 of the 5 years I ran the empowerment group, students became so interested in the concept of affective education that we formed YPAR research teams to investigate further. The first of these teams used the visual arts to explore mental health, the second conducted a mixed methods study on the state of feminism at Barnwood, and the third presented workshops on affective education to gifted youth at the state governor's school.

I maintained an equal opportunity approach and always included any young woman who wanted to participate in the groups. This meant that students sometimes joined our group mid-semester; some self-selected, others were recruited by their peers, and still others had a teacher refer them. High-achieving and gifted young men were also sometimes interested in our group. Occasionally I ran parallel sessions, one week exploring healthy relationships with the young women and the next week exploring this same topic with the young men. Each time I did this, I was struck by the similarity between the two dialogues. The last YPAR team invited a few of the young men in their class to copresent with them in their outreach presentations on navigating the transition from high school to college. At one of these presentations, Alan shared,

It's tough, guys. You apply. You hope. You wait. You get rejection notices, and then you go cry in your bedroom. We all do it; it's okay. And then after a while you realize that maybe that college wasn't the right one for you.

Alan's courageous disclosure had a powerful impact on everyone in the room. The utility of Wholehearted Teaching as a framework for broader student populations is an area I would like to explore in my future research.

Integrate Self-Care Into Your Classroom Environment

In order to implement Wholehearted Teaching, educators must be willing to talk openly about the importance of getting enough sleep, cultivating healthy relationships, eating nutritious foods, staying hydrated, practicing gratitude, and utilizing positive approaches to mitigate stress. We also must create the conditions that make these practices possible in our classrooms, so that students don't have to choose between well-being and achievement. Each year, I worked with our highest-achieving young women to bring more intentionality around self-care. We worked on positive self-talk, nutrition, fitness, gratitude, sleep, breathing, and laughter. I asked students to name their emotions, challenges, and celebrations. Collectively, we encouraged each other to be proactive, positive, and gentle with ourselves. As a team, we held each other accountable for practicing self-care and supported one another when doing so was challenging. For extensive information on self-care, see Chapter 5.

Make Storytelling Part of Your School Community

Stories have the capacity to build bridges across difference. They are a common denominator across the human condition. They have been used to illustrate, teach, entertain, and bring people together. As we consider the conditions for a wholehearted classroom culture, it is imperative that we include space for storytelling. In this research project, our storytelling work continued in the feminist tradition of viewing personal stories as powerful political and ideological tools. We were incredibly fortunate to have a partnership with Making Waves, a youth radio initiative, which gave us a public literacy platform to engage in story sharing with our community.

EXCERPT FROM CLAUDIA'S RADIO STORY
Senior in High School

May 2015

Right now, I am the only girl in my electronics class of 20 students. I feel like I need to make them feel comfortable around me because I am a woman. I try to only talk about topics I know the guys are interested in, and I stop myself from talking about some of the things I like. I never talk to them about shoes. And I love to talk about shoes.

As I transition to college and then into the workforce, I believe it will be more of the same. Women are not choosing to go into or stay in STEM fields: science, technology, engineering and math. And my question is: Why?

Claudia used her personal experiences to develop a story on the larger issue of underrepresentation of women in STEM. In her story, she identified a tension between buying into the dominant storyline ("I love to talk about shoes") while also wanting to counter the dominant storyline ("I am the only girl in my electronics class"). In our team dialogues, we explored how our lived experiences often exist within tension. For Claudia, identifying as a woman and a scientist was both messy and personal. Telling her story in an honest way that acknowledged this messiness humanized her narrative. Humanizing the complicated ways we understood youth culture and identity was precisely the aim of our radio workshops. The stories we shared were personally and politically charged. The following is an excerpt from Melissa's radio story about her relationship with both her mother and her Chinese culture.

EXCERPT FROM MELISSA'S RADIO STORY
Senior in High School

May 2015

When I was really young, I had a chore we called *sai yifu*. This meant I would lug out our wet laundry to my back patio, and hang them to dry on the clotheslines we strung up. This was one of my favorite activities to do when I was very young. But *sai yifu* also became my first experience with shame about my Chinese heritage.

Over the years, I began to dread this chore more than anything else. I grew up in a well-off and mainly White neighborhood. Nobody else I knew had to hang their clothes to dry. When asked to *sai yifu*, I would do anything to get out of it. And when that didn't work, I used to wait until nighttime to sneak out and begin. Looking back, I realize that much of my childhood was dominated by a constant, inescapable sense of shame.

It wasn't just *sai yifu*. I quickly learned to be embarrassed by almost everything about me. I wore shirts with Chinese words on them, I sometimes brought rice and seaweed for lunch, and my parents frequently clashed with everyone from PTA moms to waiters. I was ashamed of the lingering bits of my Chinese heritage I couldn't "shake off" to fit in.

Melissa struggled with this story and revised it many times. She wanted to temper her disclosure in a way that still valued her relationships with her family. Melissa navigated a fuzzy line between disclosure as courage and disclosure as shame. She often turned to the student researchers, me, and our readings on wholehearted living (Brown, 2010, 2012, 2015) to negotiate that line with both honesty and grace.

The students knew that being vulnerable was emotionally risky. However, they also believed that being courageous was a precondition for affecting change. In fact, as we analyzed the concept of emotional fortitude, we found that accepting risk (e.g., judgment and changed relationships) was part of the inherent connection between vulnerability and strength. Through courageous storytelling, the student researchers offered counter-hegemonic stories that both complicated and unmasked the affective crisis for high-achieving young women. In one of our group dialogues, Faith shared,

> I decided to talk about my struggle with anorexia, and the reason I decided to talk about that was twofold. First, talking about what I've been through, and what I'm still going through, helps me to deal with it and to process it. And second, I think one of the hardest things for me is that anorexia is really misunderstood. And so many people who go through it feel shamed into not talking about it. So if me telling my story makes them feel like, "Oh, hey, she doesn't feel ashamed of talking about it, I shouldn't feel ashamed of talking about it, there's nothing to be ashamed of," then my story will have accomplished its goal.

To date, the radio stories from this research team have reached more than 2,000 listeners, and they continue to receive weekly hits and engagements. We have heard from students, parents, teachers, and other community members that our stories "struck a chord."

Honor Nuance

Fostering a wholehearted classroom culture centers on positive relationship building (Delpit, 2006; Erwin, 2010). Each relationship is unique; each class contextualized. As an educational leader working with gifted youth, particularly young women, I was familiar with certain patterns of anxiety and pressure. Some of the challenging experiences the student researchers experienced were gendered (hooks, 2000) and raced (Collins, 2000; Hartlep, 2013). These included bullying, violence, discrimination, and exclusion. We experienced different ways that our multiple identities, including age, ability, religion, and sexual orientation, were products of systems of advantage and disadvantage (Anthias, 2008; Collins, 2000; Crenshaw, 1989, 1991). However, no two groups, stories, or experiences were the same.

Although I had planned for difficult conversations, I had not planned on how powerful it would be to participate in those conversations. I knew that in some cases, the difficult emotions our high-achieving students were processing were the product of the social-emotional vulnerabilities of being gifted youth (Dabrowski, 1967; Lovecky, 2011). The more openly we shared our personal stories and talked about identity, privilege, and challenge, the more nuanced our understanding of identity and deeper our sense of community became. Students need teachers who are willing to connect, celebrate, weep, and worry from a place of compassion. All relationships carry a level of emotional risk, and through this research, I learned that these risks are often what lead to the emotional rewards of connection and healing. However, teacher training (and teacher support) at the secondary and especially the higher education level does little to prepare instructors to build or process these deep learning relationships.

Continued Support During the College Transition

The need for compassionate and connected teachers continues into higher education. Our project supported the research that gifted and high-achieving young women have different, and often more intense, affective needs than their peers (Colangelo, 2003; Daniels & Piechowski, 2009; Kerr, 1994; Lovecky, 2011; Rimm, 1999). It further affirmed the need for affective education in schools in general, and in gifted and high-stress programs in particular (Ferguson, 2006; NAGC, 2014; Robbins, 2006). As our project developed, I noticed we had transformed our notion of the precipice. Although it was still associated with risk and fear, we now also spoke of hope and leaping into new possibilities. When I asked the student researchers about this, they shared that our research themes of courage, connection, and self-care caused them to view the precipice experience with hope and exhilaration, instead of only doubt and fear. The student researchers advocated for more gifted education groups and college counseling that encourage courage, connection, and self-care.

As teachers and counselors work to support high-achieving students, I hope this research on Wholehearted Teaching will provide a framework to help manage social-emotional vulnerabilities (Ferguson, 2006) and find meaning during this emotional transition. However, this support cannot stop at high school commencement. This study sheds new light on how college advisors and faculty might think about higher education transition programs. Our research suggests that instead of looking only at readiness and remediation, colleges also ought to put programs in place to target affective support for high-achieving students. Our project points to the powerful potential a teacher can have in connecting with vulnerable students. We know that this connection does not happen by accident.

A Message for Educators

Why do we need Wholehearted Teaching? The short answer is that challenge is unavoidable. The longer answer is that courage is the force that drives our world forward. Our students (and teachers) face a wide array of challenges. We face personal challenges, such as an ill parent or a tough soccer game. We face school challenges, such as peer pressure and high-stakes assessments. We face community challenges, such as violence and poverty. We face global challenges, such as war and hunger. Sometimes challenges are outside of our control; however, how we respond to them is always within our control, as is how we teach young people to face the challenges before them.

What does it mean to face something with courage? Often, I think we mistake courage for physical strength, valor, power, and guardedness. It turns out that these things have little to do with courage. The word *courage* comes from the Latin word *cor*, meaning "heart." Brené Brown (2007), a social work scholar and vulnerability researcher, reminded us in her work, that courage is "a heart word." It literally means "of the heart." In my conversations with students, we often talk about making the difficult but "right" choice to take an action that our conscience tells us to take, but that our heart says is going to be hard—telling a young person that his joke isn't funny but offensive; leading a class discussion after a tragedy; comforting someone who has lost a family member; calling children's services.

We've all experienced these moments. Life is a series of these moments. Negotiating them with grace builds up our emotional strength, something my students called *strong vulnerability*. It is inherently difficult to speak truth to power, truth to bullies, truth to self. This difficulty, this vulnerability, is often indicative of change potential. When we take the risk and make the hard but right choice, we often see great rewards, such as stronger connections, safer schools and communities, and more courageous peer groups. When courage becomes part of the classroom culture, courageous acts are contagious.

The reason courage is an emotional experience is because it is closely related to fear, so let's look at that word, too. In Hebrew there are distinct words for two different kinds of fear (Mohr, 2015). These words are *pachad* and *yirah*. Pachad is the fear we imagine. It is often irrational, limiting, and dark. It includes fear of ridicule. Yirah, on the other hand, translates roughly to "awe," and it comes from the word for God. It is the fear that overcomes us when we are in the midst of something grand, when we are working with flow, when we realize we have gone from dreaming big to living (or learning) big—even if only for a moment.

In schools, we want to limit fear of ridicule, bullying, and exclusion. But awe is something else entirely. We want students to lose themselves in a work of art, to stand amazed at the global connections surrounding contemporary issues like water quality or access to education; we want their pulse to quicken before they say something brave. Further, we want to normalize the emotional experience of being courageous so that our students can become more adept at drawing on their own inner heart strength. Students need opportunities to become proficiently courageous.

We do not always get to choose the mountains we climb or the precipices our students come to on their journeys. However, we can choose our outlooks and our action plans. I want our students to feel in control of both of these. Sometimes the challenges our students face are well outside of their sphere of influence. Sometimes life is unfair. In these moments, more than ever, we need courage, connection, and self-care. How much time do we spend in schools talking about heart strength? How many class discussions do we have about agency, empathy, and compassion (including self-compassion)?

Teaching is heart-heavy work; sometimes our students bring in heavy things. When they do, we need to help them respond from their heart, meaning with courage; we need to give young people permission to lean into their emotions, to feel deeply, and to find inner strength. Being effective in these tough situations requires exactly the same skill set for teachers. You need to respond from your heart, give yourself permission to listen, acknowledge, hold space, and find the inner strength to guide young people forward. Imagine schools where students are taught to respond to adversity with strength and love. In such schools, I believe we would experience healthier and stronger relationships and bolder and more effective solutions to problems.

CHAPTER 8

Coming Home

Title

Cultivating a Sense of Home in Our Classrooms, Educator Showcase (2018)

Participant Notes (Stephanie Walter, educational leader):

The mother's voice saying, "Honey, how are you? I can tell from your face that something is wrong." Empathetic. Strong. Wise. Giver of advice and soother with food in all its forms. Comfort. All-consuming love. This was home. A dad's voice saying, "When you fight, keep your wrists straight, kid," and "Don't get married too young," and "You can be anything you set your mind to." Strong arms and a stronger heart. Writer of poetry. Reader of scripture. Doer of heroic deeds. This was home.

The daughter grows up. She moves away. She never comes back. Not really, not ever to stay. Instead, she is searching and escaping and growing and exploring.

The opening image for this chapter was taken at the showcase for my most recent professional development series. This series centered on the idea of cultivating a sense of home in our classrooms. Around 20 educators participated in the project. Together we explored home as nuanced, layered, and deeply important to school communities. At the close of the series, each of the educators presented original works of art explaining their personal definitions of home. They also shared courageous vignettes and poems about how these definitions have evolved over time. In this final chapter, I want to build on these ideas about home.

Home is where our story starts. In many ways Wholehearted Teaching is about cultivating a sense of home in our schools. Like the other themes we've explored through this research, home is complicated. Our lived experiences around home are rarely easy or simple. Our students bring a range of complex ideas about home to school. There we have the opportunity and responsibility to validate their experiences, forge new communities, build safe spaces, and let young people know they belong in our classrooms. In this delicate work, how do we negotiate the heavy and light, the happy and the sad, the tactile and the abstract? How can we heal some of the pain our students bring with them? To my surprise, art was an answer to some of these questions.

When I first started teaching in gifted education, I was surprised to find so many of our highest-achieving young women enamored with the art room. I quickly learned that if my students weren't in the gifted room or at an extracurricular activity, there was a good chance I could find them in the art studio—creating. My curiosity about this led to the YPAR group that created our *Perspectives on the Precipice* series. Molly, one of the student researchers, told me,

> Art is a mode of communication that is unique to every other. There are so many subtle details that can be used to convey a message in art: from color scheme and texture to subject matter and lighting. In art, mistakes don't exist. . . . The process of making art can be mindless, which can prove to be very telling when a piece becomes an outlet for one's stream of consciousness. And when it does, it serves to be both therapeutic and aesthetic. Why art? Art exposes the soul of the artist.

Through art, Sasha was able to speak back to a culture that expected her to present herself in specific gendered ways. Jana created a postmodern feminist piece on the expectations of student athletes. Ashley created a vibrant piece on the way pressure and institutions attempted to minimize her experiences. Norah's self-portrait is startling in its use of shadows. The visual literacies the student researchers used to share these ideas added a complexity that wouldn't have been possible with just text. As I learned new lessons about audio and listening through our work with radio, I also learned new lessons about light and dark through our work with paint and canvas.

The more I saw how art gave students new tools to process, express, and create, the more committed I became to integrating art into my teaching practice. This felt like a risk, as I don't think of myself as an artist. I can't draw a realistic horse, correctly shade a three-dimensional object, or apply color theory to a project. Despite these limitations, I have now successfully led both student and teacher groups in art projects and creative showcases. The strategies I used to engage in this work should be no surprise. I leaned on the community experts around me, both student and professional. My friend, Sharyn, an extraordinarily talented artist, helped me think differently about my ability to integrate art into my teaching practice. We meet at coffee shops for brainstorm sessions when I have a challenge I think can best be explored through art. She's invited me into her home to paint in her personal studio, and she's gently reminded me when I am going to need extra super glue for an upcoming project.

Healing

Healing is not synonymous with "getting over" our challenges or pains. Instead, with each iteration of our central stories, we found small ways to be kinder, gentler, or more positive with ourselves. Again and again, I was struck by the disclosure of the bright young women I worked with. I was inspired by this disclosure not only for the courage it represented, although that was certainly admirable, but also for the ways the students' vulnerability bolstered our ability to move forward. By working honestly and openly through challenge, we found tremendous moments of inner strength and healing (Daniels & Piechowski, 2009; Lovecky, 2011). During the course of this project, we all experienced physical or emotional healing (and for some, both). Through courage, connection, and self-care we noticed that over time we felt less isolated and hurt, and more connected and grounded.

For example, although Leslie still experienced times of doubt, by the end of our project, she found she was also better able to identify her strengths.

Faith shared that although she knew she still had a distorted body image, she was now able to embrace the fact that she continued to maintain a healthy weight. Elaine made peace with herself and her best friend. Melissa developed a self-care practice that gave her the strength to enroll in her dream school and move away from her mother and sister. At the onset of the project, all of these accomplishments would have seemed unlikely or even impossible.

We celebrated the inner strength each of us found through living our stories, including the difficult and messier parts of those personal narratives. Revisiting and revising our central stories through writing, dialogue, and practice led to a kind of healing. For us, healing often meant forgiving each other, or more often ourselves, for mistakes and imperfections (Brown, 2010). We learned to view our central stories holistically, as both/and narratives that are messy, complex, rich, and living. Story sharing and connection helped us cultivate the resilience (Brown, 2012, 2015) we needed to embrace those stories and move forward with strength and understanding.

Keeping My Office Door Open

By the summer of 2015, the student researchers had all moved on to their postsecondary journeys. The first empowerment class had graduated from college, and the last class was beginning. I had also moved on from Barnwood and into my current position in educational administration. Although their messages come less regularly, most of the student researchers have continued to stay in touch. They stop by to see me on their fall and spring breaks. They text me links to articles or books that are relevant to our work and comment on my social media posts. Every year, a few of the students go quiet. At first, I wondered if they had "outgrown" their need for our group and my guidance. And a few of them had; they found other mentors and other relationships that met their needs for connection. This is part of the ebb and flow of life. However, I've learned that if I am patient, most of the students resurface, sometimes showing up at my office unannounced or other times sending me thoughtful e-mails on their upcoming adventures. We sit together over coffee or message on our phones. They share stories from study abroad adventures, medical school applications, and volunteer work in public schools.

During the first crisp days of 2016, the last group of student researchers sent a message to our former group chat to schedule a meeting for coffee.

We met downtown at a crowded coffee shop and talked for 2 hours without pausing. We were so engaged in conversation that most of us forgot to even buy coffee. I felt a bit guilty about this so I went back the next day, bought a latte, and surprised myself by writing this poem.

Encouragingly Yours
A poem for my students

You are lovely. You see the world,
not for all that is wrong, but for all
that might be right, or beautiful,
or possible.

Your enthusiasm is contagious.
When you come to class, you
can't help but make an entrance.

You care deeply about big important
things. You also care deeply about small
important things. Keep caring.

Your naivety is endearing. You tell me
you are going to change injustice with a
single story, a conversation, a class . . .
I smile, because I can't help myself.

"Teacher, I know it's only a start,
but we have to start somewhere,
so let's start today." I wouldn't dream
of arguing with you.

You cannot remember a time before cell
phones, Google, or social media. When
you tell me we are all connected, I nod,
because, of course, you're correct.

You believe it, too. I see you there,
on campus, building a new world.
Hold fast to that hope and faster still
to each other.

I hadn't seen Naomi in almost 3 years when she dropped by my office one day before her last semester at an Ivy League college. When she was in high school, Naomi designed and edited our gifted education newsletters, announcements, and flyers. I looked up from my computer where I was working on a data report on school achievement. I was struggling with formatting my report and couldn't get the bullet points to align. Naomi laughed, came right behind my computer, took my mouse, and fiddled with the formatting until all of the bullets lined up straight. I thanked her and said we should take a walk. We walked downtown for a little more than an hour, both of us wearing high heels not made for long walks. Naomi was trying to decide what to do after college. She was interested in environmental sustainability, but given the recent backlash on environmental law and protections, she wasn't sure this was the opportune moment for her to find a position in that field. She was interested in graduate school. She had also already received a job offer in consulting. I listened, struck by the fact that there we were walking together and discussing another huge precipice. Life is cyclical.

Recently, I heard from two former students; one is a gifted writer and recent college graduate, and the other a gifted musician and sophomore in college. Both students participated in our empowerment group, although neither joined a research team. Their attendance at our luncheons was a bit sporadic. I was surprised and very happy to hear from them. The first told me she was interviewing for a teaching position in gifted education. She asked if we could talk on the phone. We talked for the better part of an hour about her interest in equity and empowerment. We talked about the role of affective supports for gifted youth. We talked about issues surrounding access at the inner-city school where she was currently student teaching. Whether or not she pursues a career in gifted education, I know she will be an amazing teacher. The second student told me she was part of a high-achieving women's group on her college campus. She was reaching out because she saw many of the issues we had worked on in our high school group affecting her new peers. She mentioned healthy relationships, self-care, and balance as areas where they could use more support. She asked if I would meet with her group. I smiled and told her, "Absolutely."

Humanizing Exiting

MY JOURNAL
Kathryn

August 2015*

Elaine has to leave our meeting first. Before she does, we take a group photo. The sun is just starting to set; it throws golden light across us. The student researchers linger, not yet ready to say goodbye. It is a hot summer day in August. We visit in a circle, laughing and holding on for a few more minutes. I thank the students and tell them how lucky I was to work with them. We were all so fortunate to work and learn together. We make tentative agreements for quick final updates before they leave for college. I assure the students I'm always just a text, e-mail, or Facebook message away. We hug and say goodbye for now.

*A few days before the last student research group left for college.

It turned out that "for now" was pretty short. Four days after our final team celebration, Leslie texted me asking if I had any more yarn for the scarf she was knitting, so I brought some by her house. A couple of days later, she messaged me again asking if we could go for a trail walk together. We walked for hours talking about college, self-care, relationships, and saying goodbye. The following week, Faith asked if I would meet her for frozen yogurt. I recognized what a privilege these requests were. In these second "final" dialogues, we all talked about home. Home surfaced in the small details. The student researchers spoke of Friday night football games, their mothers' cooking, a favorite ice cream shop, and a cup of chamomile tea with a trusted teacher. It seemed that home was made of these things (Fishman-Weaver, 2016).

As a research team, we did not practice courage by defeating monsters; instead, we practiced courage by sharing personal stories. We shared things we had not shared before. We discovered that personal stories were both humanizing and healing. It is vital that young people have a support group to process, share, and celebrate with. We practiced connection in the positive peer group of our research team and with trusted adult mentors. We practiced self-care through laughter, fitness, healthy eating, deep breathing, and saying "no thank you" to adding yet another obligation to our overloaded schedules.

Humanizing exiting is a newer topic in humanizing research (Figueroa, 2014). It refers to ending studies and research projects with thoughtfulness and intention. The communities formed during collaborative research matter, and when these projects come to a close, that process is significant as well. When I met with Leslie and then Faith for those extra "final" visits before they left for college, it was an exercise in all of our research themes: courage, connection, and self-care. I listened to more stories of school, college, family, fear, hope, identity, and growth. I beamed with pride at their new sense of adventure, even as I empathized with their many apprehensions.

The Expansive Properties of Home

Leslie was concerned that her sense of home would evaporate as her friends boarded planes or drove away in cars piled high with clothes, blankets, and rolled-up posters. She worried they would never return to this same home again. As usual, the student researchers were right. They will never return to this same constellation of people, emotions, and experiences again.

That afternoon when Faith and I visited over frozen yogurt, I realized that *exiting* is a kind of a misnomer. Yes, the student researchers left; they moved on to other adventures, precipices, crises, challenges, and celebrations. Yet, our relationships and lessons from this research have continued. I look forward to the student researchers "coming home" over winter break. It is always good to get together to talk over food, to share our joys and challenges, and to laugh. I have been thinking a lot about home lately. I know that in charting my own course through this curvy road called life, home has become larger, not smaller.

When the students come back to this place on the map, we go to an ice cream shop or a pizza parlor. They tell me about how the ice cream shops and pizza places on their campuses have different ingredients and quirks than the ones we have here. During their summer break, we talk about how hot it is and marvel at the fireflies.

"My college friends call them lightning bugs."

At homecoming, the leaves turn orange and gold, and sometimes we meet up at a football game. During winter break, I make us hot chocolate and we talk about how cold it is.

"It is! Although, you can't even imagine how cold it is in Boston!"

Sometimes one of the students texts me over spring break and we meet up for a soggy walk on the trail.

Our work around Wholehearted Teaching gave us the confidence to leap forward with arms wide open. It also gave us the knowledge that although such leaps are risky, the risks of being closed off are even greater. In the last couple of months while finalizing this manuscript, I have gotten calls and texts from many of the student researchers. They tell me they miss their friends, their mothers, and our research team. They also tell me about new friends and new groups that matter to them. They tell me that their classes are challenging them and that they continue to worry about their ability to be successful. They are looking forward to new adventures in school, such as studying a new language or beginning law school. Many of them want to see new places; they are applying for graduate schools, volunteer initiatives, and programs to teach abroad. Last summer, one of the student researchers got married.

They have made friends, found mentors, and are pursuing new and inspiring adventures. They are building connections through owning and sharing their personal stories. They continue to come upon precipices, some of which are scary and big. Usually, though, they find the emotional strength to look out across that landscape of life and move forward. As they keep moving forward, authoring their own stories, I hope they realize that wherever they are, they are home.

References

Adichie, C. N. (2009). *The danger of a single story* [Video file]. Retrieved from https://www.ted.com/talks/chimamanda_adichie_the_danger_ of_a_single_story

Adichie, C. N. (2014). *We should all be feminists.* New York, NY: Vintage.

Amen, J., & Reglin, G. (1992). High school seniors tell why they are "stressed out." *The Clearing House, 66,* 27–29.

Amend, E. (2009). Dabrowski's theory: Possibilities and implications of misdiagnosis, missed diagnosis, and dual diagnosis in gifted individuals. In S. Daniels & M. M. Piechowski (Eds.), *Living with intensity: Understanding the sensitivity, excitability, and emotional development of gifted children, adolescents, and adults* (pp. 83–104). Scottsdale, AZ: Great Potential Press.

American Association of University Women. (2018). *The simple truth about the gender pay gap.* Retrieved from https://www.aauw.org/resource/ the-simple-truth-about-the-gender-pay-gap

Anderson, E. (1995). Feminist epistemology: An interpretation and a defense. *Hypatia, 10*(3), 50–84.

Anthias, F. (2008). Thinking through the lens of translocational positionality: An intersectionality frame for understanding identity and belonging. *Translocations: Migration and Social Change, 4*(1), 5–20.

Appadurai, A. (2006). The right to research. *Globalization, Societies, and Education, 4,* 167–177.

Beauvoir, S. (1974). *The second sex.* New York, NY: Vintage Books.

Belenky, M., Clinchy, B., Goldberg, N., & Tarule, J. (1997). *Women's ways of knowing: the development of self, voice, and mind.* New York, NY: Basic Books.

Bell, M., McLaughlin, M., & Sequeira, J. (2002). Discrimination, harassment, and the glass ceiling: Women executives as change agents. *Journal of Business Ethics, 37,* 65–76.

Belsey, C. (2002). *Poststructuralism: A very short introduction.* New York, NY: Oxford University Press.

Beyer, L. E. (2002). The politics of standardization: Teacher education in the USA. *Journal of Education for Teaching, 28,* 239–245.

Block, A. A. (2008). Why should I be a teacher? *Journal of Teacher Education, 59,* 416–427.

Bloom, B. (Ed.). (1956). *Taxonomy of educational objectives: The classification of educational goals. Handbook I: Cognitive domain.* New York, NY: Longmans Green.

Blum, L. A. (1988). Gilligan and Kohlberg: Implications for moral theory. *Ethics, 98,* 472–491.

Bolman, L. G., & Deal, T. E. (2013). *Reframing organizations: Artistry, choice, and leadership* (5th ed.). San Francisco, CA: Jossey-Bass.

Boyer, E. L. (1986). Smoothing the transition from school to college. *Phi Delta Kappan, 68,* 283–287.

Brown, B. (2007). *I thought it was just me (but it isn't): Making the journey from "What will people think?" to "I am enough."* New York, NY: Avery.

Brown, B. (2010). *The gifts of imperfection: Let go of who you think you're supposed to be and embrace who you are.* Center City, MN: Hazelden.

Brown, B. (2012). *Daring greatly: How the courage to be vulnerable transforms the way we live, love, parent, and lead.* New York, NY: Gotham.

Brown, B. (2015). *Rising strong: How the ability to reset transforms the way we live, love, parent, and lead.* New York, NY: Penguin Random House.

Butler, J. (1990). *Gender trouble.* New York, NY: Routledge.

Butler, J. (2006). Performative acts and gender constitution: An essay in phenomenology and feminist theory. In M. Arnot & M. Mac an Ghaill (Eds.), *The RoutledgeFalmer reader in gender and education* (pp. 73–83). New York, NY: Routledge.

Butler, J. (2015). *Senses of the subject.* New York, NY: Fordham University Press.

Cannella, G. S., & Lincoln, Y. S. (2011). Ethics, research regulations, and critical social science. In N. K. Denzin & Y. S. Lincoln (Eds.), *The SAGE handbook of qualitative research* (4th ed., pp. 81–90). Thousand Oaks, CA: SAGE.

Charmaz, K. (2014). *Constructing grounded theory* (2nd ed.). Thousand Oaks, CA: SAGE.

Chua, A. (2011). *Battle hymn of the tiger mother*. New York, NY: Penguin.

Clance, P. R., & Imes, S. A. (1978). The imposter phenomenon in high achieving women: Dynamics and therapeutic intervention. *Psychotherapy: Theory, Research & Practice, 15,* 241–247.

Cohn, S. (2002). Gifted students who are gay, lesbian, or bisexual. In M. Neihart, S. M. Reis, N. M. Robinson, & S. M. Moon (Eds.), *The social and emotional development of gifted children: What do we know?* (pp. 145–155). Waco, TX: Prufrock Press.

Colangelo, N. (2003). Counseling gifted students. In N. Colangelo & G. Davis, *The handbook of gifted education* (3rd ed., pp. 373–387). Boston, MA: Pearson.

Collins, P. (2000). *Black feminist thought*. New York, NY: Routledge.

Collins, P. (2013). Black feminist thought in the matrix of domination. In C. Lemert (Ed.), *Social theory: The multicultural, global, and classic readings* (5th ed., pp. 403–411). Boulder, CO: Westview Press.

Collins, P. H. (1998). It's all in the family: Intersections of gender, race, and nation. *Hypatia, 13*(3), 62–82.

Crenshaw, K. (1989). Demarginalizing the intersection of race and sex: A black feminist critique of antidiscrimination doctrine, feminist theory and antiracist politics. *The University of Chicago Legal Forum, 140,* 139–167.

Crenshaw, K. (1991). Mapping the margins: Intersectionality, identity politics and violence against women of color. *Stanford Law Review, 46,* 1241–1299.

Creswell, J. W., & Miller, D. L. (2000). Determining validity in qualitative inquiry. *Theory Into Practice, 39,* 124–130.

Crotty, M. (1998). *The foundations of social research: Meaning and perspective in the research process*. Thousand Oaks, CA: SAGE.

Dabrowski, K. (1964). *Positive disintegration*. Boston, MA: Little, Brown.

Dabrowski, K. (1967). *Personality-shaping through positive disintegration*. Boston, MA: Little, Brown.

Dabrowski, K. (1970). *Mental growth through positive disintegration*. London, England: Gryf.

Dabrowski, K., & Piechowski, M. (1977). *Theory of levels of emotional development: Multilevelness and positive disintegration* (Vol. 2). Oceanside, NY: Dabor Science.

Daniels, S., & Piechowski, M. M. (2009). *Living with intensity: Understanding the sensitivity, excitability, and emotional development of gifted children, adolescents, and adults.* Scottsdale, AZ: Great Potential Press.

Delpit, L. (2006). *Other people's children: Cultural conflict in the classroom.* New York, NY: The New Press.

Di Cintio, M. (2015). For gifted children, being intelligent can have dark implications. *Calgary Herald.* Retrieved from https://calgaryherald.com/life/swerve/gifted-children-are-frequently-misunderstood

DuFour R., DuFour, R., & Eaker R. (2008). *Revisiting professional learning communities at work: New insights for improving schools.* Bloomington, IN: Solution Tree Press.

Dweck, C. (2006). *Mindset: The new psychology of success.* New York, NY: Ballantine Books.

Elliott, J. (1991). *Action research for educational change: Developing teachers and teaching.* Buckingham, England: Open University Press.

Erwin, J. C. (2010). *Inspiring the best in students.* Alexandria, VA: ASCD.

Ferguson, S. A. K. (2006, Winter). A case for affective education: Addressing the social and emotional needs of gifted students in the classroom. *Virginia Association for the Gifted Newsletter,* 1–3.

Fiedler, E. (1999). Gifted children: The promise of potential/the problems of potential. In V. L. Schwean & D. H. Saklofske (Eds.), *Handbook of psychosocial characteristics of exceptional children* (pp. 401–441). New York, NY: Plenum.

Figueroa, A. M. (2014). La carta de responsabilidad: The problem of departure. In D. Paris & M. T. Winn (Eds.), *Humanizing research: Decolonizing qualitative inquiry with youth and communities* (pp. 129–146). Thousand Oaks, CA: SAGE.

Fishman-Weaver, K. (2014). The continued importance of high school personnel's support in the high-school-to-college transition. *American Journal of Education Forum.* Retrieved from https://www.ajeforum.com/the-continued-importance-of-high-school-personnels-support-in-the-high-school-to-college-transition-by-kathryn-fishman-weaver

Fishman-Weaver, K. (2015). Gifted education as safe space: An equal opportunity model. *American Journal of Education Forum.* Retrieved from http://www.ajeforum.com/gifted-education-as-safe-space-an-equal-opportunity-model-by-kathryn-fishman-weaver

Fishman-Weaver, K. (2016). The expansive properties of home during times of transition. *The Columbia Missourian.* Retrieved from https://www.columbiamissourian.com/from_readers/from-readers-the-expansive-properties-of-home-during-times-of/article_12a53ab0-562f-11e5-82b0-93b8c9326f00.html

Ford, D. Y., & Grantham, T. C. (2003). Providing access for culturally diverse gifted students: From deficit to dynamic thinking. *Theory Into Practice, 42,* 217–225.

Gilligan, C. (1982). *In a different voice: Psychological theory and women's development.* Boston, MA: Harvard University Press.

Gilligan, C., Ward, J., Taylor, J., & Bardige, B. (Eds.). (1988). *Mapping the moral domain: A contribution of women's thinking to psychological theory and education.* Cambridge, MA: Harvard University Press.

Gramsci, A. (2013). Intellectuals and hegemony. In C. Lemert (Ed.), *Social theory: The multicultural, global, and classic readings* (5th ed., p. 202). Boulder, CO: Westview Press.

Gross, M. U. M. (2002). Social and emotional issues for exceptionally intellectually gifted students. In M. Neihart, S. M. Reis, N. M. Robinson, & S. M. Moon (Eds.), *The social and emotional development of gifted children: What do we know?* (pp. 17–30). Waco, TX: Prufrock Press.

Grzanka, P. (2014). *Intersectionality: A foundations and frontiers reader.* Boulder, CO: Westview Press.

Guillemin, M., & Gillam, L. (2004). Ethics, reflexivity, and "ethically important moments" in research. *Qualitative Inquiry, 10,* 261–280.

Hanley, S. J., & Abell, S. C. (2002). Maslow and relatedness: Creating an interpersonal model of self-actualization. *Journal of Humanistic Psychology, 42*(4), 37–57.

Hartlep, N. D. (2013). The model minority? *Diverse Issues in Higher Education, 30*(2), 14.

Heron, J., & Reason, P. (2001). The practice of co-operative inquiry: Research "with" rather than "on" people. In P. Reason & H. Bradbury (Eds.), *Handbook of action research: Participative inquiry and practice* (pp. 179–188). Thousand Oaks, CA: SAGE.

Hesse-Biber, S. N. (2012). Feminist research: Exploring, interrogating, and transforming the interconnections of epistemology, methodology, and method. In S. N. Hesse-Biber (Ed.), *The handbook of feminist research: Theory and praxis* (2nd ed., pp. 2–26). Thousand Oaks, CA: SAGE.

Hoge, R. D., & Renzulli, J. S. (1993). Exploring the link between giftedness and self-concept. *Review of Educational Research, 63,* 449–465.

hooks, b. (1994). *Teaching to transgress: Education as the practice of freedom.* New York, NY: Routledge.

hooks, b. (2000). *Feminism is for everybody: Passionate politics.* Cambridge, England: South End Press.

Hoy, W. K., Tarter, J., & Hoy, A. W. (2006). Academic optimism of schools: A force for student achievement. *American Educational Research Journal, 43,* 425–446.

Huitt, W. (2007). Maslow's hierarchy of needs. *Educational Psychology Interactive.* Valdosta, GA: Valdosta State University.

Irizarry, J., & Brown, T. (2014). Humanizing research in dehumanizing spaces: The challenges and opportunities of conducting participatory action research with youth in schools. In D. Paris & M. T. Winn (Eds.), *Humanizing research: Decolonizing qualitative inquiry with youth and communities* (pp. 63–80). Thousand Oaks, CA: SAGE.

James, E. A., Milenkiewicz, M. T., & Bucknam, A. (2008). *Participatory action research for educational leadership: Using data-driven decision making to improve schools.* Thousand Oaks, CA: SAGE.

Kaye P. (2012). *Why we tell stories* [Video file]. Retrieved from https://www.youtube.com/watch?v=s7fWagDQyvg

Kerr, B. A. (1994). *Smart girls two: A new psychology of girls, women and giftedness.* Dayton, OH: Psychology Press.

Kerr, B. A., & Foley Nicpon, M. (2003). Gender and giftedness. In N. Colangelo & G. Davis (Eds.), *The handbook of gifted education* (3rd ed., pp. 493–506). Boston, MA: Pearson.

Kezar, A. J., Carducci, R., & Contreras-McGavin, M. (2006). *Rethinking the "l" word in higher education: The revolution of research on leadership.* San Francisco, CA: Wiley.

Kindlon, D. (2006). *Alpha girls: Understanding the new American girl and how she is changing the world.* New York, NY: Rodale.

Kinloch, V., & San Pedro, T. (2014). The space between listening and storying: Foundations for projects in humanization. In D. Paris & M. T. Winn (Eds.), *Humanizing research: Decolonizing qualitative inquiry with youth and communities* (pp. 21–42). Thousand Oaks, CA: SAGE.

Kohlberg, L. (1981). *Essays on moral development: The philosophy of moral development* (Vol. 1). San Francisco, CA: Harper & Row.

Kolmar, W. K., & Bartkowski, F. (1999). *Feminist theory: A reader.* New York, NY: McGraw-Hill.

Kosciw, J. G., Greytak, E. A., Giga, N. M., Villenas, C., & Danischewski, D. J. (2016). *The 2015 national school climate survey: The experiences of lesbian, gay, bisexual, transgender, and queer youth in our nation's schools.* New York, NY: GLSEN.

Krathwohl, D. R. (2002). A revision of Bloom's taxonomy: An overview. *Theory Into Practice, 41,* 212–218.

References

Krathwohl, D. R., Bloom, B. S., & Masia, B. B. (1964). *Taxonomy of educational objectives: The classification of educational goals. Handbook II: Affective domain.* New York, NY: McKay.

Lee, C., Dickson, D. A., Conley, C. S., & Holmbeck, G. N. (2014). A closer look at self-esteem, perceived social support, and coping strategy: A prospective study of depressive symptomatology across the transition to college. *Journal of Social and Clinical Psychology, 33,* 560–585.

Lincoln, Y. S., & Guba, E. G. (1985). *Naturalistic inquiry.* Newbury Park, CA: SAGE.

Lipman, P. (2003). Chicago school policy: Regulating Black and Latino youth in the global city. *Race Ethnicity and Education, 6,* 331–355.

Lipman, P. (2004). *High stakes education: Inequality, globalization, and urban school reform.* New York, NY: Routledge.

Lorde, A. (1984). *Sister outsider.* New York, NY: Crossing Press.

Lovecky, A. (2011). Exploring social and emotional aspects of giftedness in children. *Supporting Emotional Needs of the Gifted.* Retrieved from https://sengifted.org/exploring-social-and-emotional-aspects-of-giftedness-in-children

Lubinski, D., Benbow, C., & Kell, H. (2014). Life paths and accomplishments of mathematically precocious males and females four decades later. *Psychological Science, 25,* 2217–2232.

Maguire, P. (1987). *Doing participatory research: A feminist approach.* Amherst, MA: Center for International Education.

Marshall, C., & Rossman, G. B. (2014). *Designing qualitative research* (6th ed.). Thousand Oaks, CA: SAGE.

Maslow, A. H. (1970a). *Motivation and personality.* New York, NY: Harper & Row.

Maslow, A. H. (1970b). *Religions, values, and peak experiences.* New York, NY: Penguin. (Original work published 1964)

Mathison, S., & Ross, E. W. (2002). Hegemony and "accountability" in schools and universities. *Workplace, 9,* 88–102.

Maurer, G. (2011). "I used to be gifted": Exploring potential among gifted adolescent females. In J. A. Frazier & A. D. Frazier (Eds.), *Special populations in gifted education: Understanding our most able students from diverse backgrounds* (pp. 195–223). Waco, TX: Prufrock Press.

McIntyre, A. (2008). Participatory action research. In J. Van Maanen (Series Ed.), *Qualitative research methods series* (Vol. 52). Thousand Oaks, CA: SAGE.

Mendaglio, S. (2002). Dabrowski's theory of positive disintegration: Some implications for teachers of gifted students. *AGATE, 15*(2), 14–22.

Miller, C. C. (2014). Even among Harvard graduates, women fall short of their work expectations. *The New York Times*. Retrieved from https://www.nytimes.com/2014/11/30/upshot/even-among-harvard-gradu-ates-women-fall-short-of-their-work-expectations.html

Mohr, T. (2015). *Playing big: Practical wisdom for women who want to speak up, create, and lead.* New York, NY: Avery.

Moon, S. M. (2002). Counseling needs and strategies. In M. Neihart, S. M. Reis, N. M. Robinson, & S. M. Moon (Eds.), *The social and emotional development of gifted children: What do we know?* (pp. 213–222). Waco, TX: Prufrock Press.

Morrell, E. (2004). *Becoming critical researchers: Literacy and empower-ment for urban youth.* New York, NY: Lang.

Myers, S. M., & Myers, C. B. (2012). Are discussions about college between parents and their high school children a college-planning activ-ity? Making the case and testing the predictors. *American Journal of Education, 118,* 281–308.

Nash, J. C. (2008). Re-thinking intersectionality. *Feminist Review, 89,* 1–15.

National Alliance on Mental Illness. (2018). *LGBTQ.* Retrieved from https://www.nami.org/find-support/lgbtq

National Association for Gifted Children. (2014). *Why are gifted programs needed?* Retrieved from https://www.nagc.org/resources-publications/gifted-education-practices/why-are-gifted-programs-needed

Neihart, M. (2016). Psychological factors in talent development. In M. Neihart, S. I. Pfeiffer, & T. L. Cross (Eds.), *The social and emotional development of gifted children: What do we know?* (2nd ed., pp. 159–172). Waco, TX: Prufrock Press.

Neumeister, K. (2016). Perfectionism in gifted students. In M. Neihart, S. I. Pfeiffer, & T. L. Cross (Eds.), *The social and emotional development of gifted children: What do we know?* (2nd ed., pp. 29–40). Waco, TX: Prufrock Press.

Nuhfer, E. (2005). De Bono's red hat on Krathwohl's head: Irrational means to rational ends—More fractal thoughts on the forbidden affective: Educating in Fractal Patterns XIII. *National Teaching and Learning Forum, 14*(5), 7–11.

Reis, S. M. (1987). We can't change what we don't recognize: Understanding the special needs of gifted females. *Gifted Child Quarterly, 31,* 83–89.

Renzulli, J. S. (2011). More changes needed to expand gifted identification and support. *Phi Delta Kappan, 92*(8), 61.

References

Rimm, S. (1999). *See Jane win: The Rimm report on how 1,000 girls became successful women.* New York, NY: Crown.

Robbins, A. (2006). *The overachievers: The secret lives of driven kids.* New York, NY: Hyperion.

Robinson, N. M., & Reis S. M. (2016). Foreword. In M. Neihart, S. I. Pfeiffer, & T. L. Cross (Eds.), *The social and emotional development of gifted children: What do we know?* (2nd ed., pp. xii–xiv). Waco, TX: Prufrock Press.

Salovey, P. (2015). Repair the world! *Office of the President, Yale University.* Retrieved from https://president.yale.edu/speeches-writings/speeches/repair-world

Schuler, P. (2002). Perfectionism in gifted children and adolescents. In M. Neihart, S. M. Reis, N. M. Robinson, & S. M. Moon (Eds.), *The social and emotional development of gifted children: What do we know?* (pp. 71–81). Waco, TX: Prufrock Press.

Shields, C. M. (2004). Dialogic leadership for social justice: Overcoming pathologies of silence. *Educational Administration Quarterly, 40,* 109–132.

Snyder, R. C. (2008). What is third-wave feminism? A new dimensions essay. *Signs, 34,* 175–196.

St. Pierre, E. A. (2000). Poststructural feminism in education: An overview. *International Journal of Qualitative Studies in Education, 13,* 477–515.

Subotnik R., Worrell, F., & Olszewski-Kublius, P. (2016). The psychological science of talent development. In M. Neihart, S. I. Pfeiffer, & T. L. Cross (Eds.), *The social and emotional development of gifted children: What do we know?* (2nd ed., pp. 145–158). Waco, TX: Prufrock Press.

Taylor, R. R., Jason, L. A., Keys, C. B., Suarez-Balcazar, Y., Davis, M. I., Durlak, J. A., & Isenberg, D. H. (2006). Introduction: Capturing theory and methodology in participatory research. In L. A. Jason, C. B. Keys, Y. Suaraz-Balcazar, R. R. Taylor, & M. I. Davis (Eds.), *Participatory community research: Theories and methods in action* (pp. 3–15). Washington, DC: American Psychological Association.

Tuck, E. (2009). Suspending damage: A letter to communities. *Harvard Educational Review, 79,* 409–428.

Vyuk, M. A., Krieshok, T. S., & Kerr, B. A. (2016). Openness to experience rather than overexcitabilities: Call it like it is. *Gifted Child Quarterly, 60,* 192–211.

Waite, D., Boone, M., & McGhee, M. (2014). A critical sociocultural view of accountability. *Journal of School Leadership, 11,* 182–203.

Will, M. (2015). Disciplines that expect 'brilliance' tend to punish women, study finds. *The Chronicle of Higher Education.* Retrieved from https://chronicle.com/article/Disciplines-That-Expect/151217

Wiseman, R. (2009). *Queen bees and wannabes: Helping your daughter survive cliques, gossip, boyfriends, and the new realities of girl world.* New York, NY: Three Rivers Press.

World Health Organization. (2018). *Constitution of WHO: Principles.* Retrieved from http://www.who.int/about/mission/en

Young, I. M. (2005). *On female body experience.* New York, NY: Oxford University Press.

Zack, N. (2005). *Inclusive feminism: A third wave theory of women's commonality.* Lanham, MD: Rowman & Littlefield.

Methodology Appendix

I am often asked how to set up youth participatory action research (YPAR) projects with student communities. Sometimes these questions are practical in nature: *How can I do similar work at my school?* Sometimes these questions are academic in nature: *How does YPAR fit within the matrix of qualitative methodologies?* Still other times, scholars want to know how feminism and YPAR can work in concert. For me, the short answer to all of these inquiries is that educators' best work happens when we spend less time talking and directing and more time listening and responding. The longer answer is outlined in this appendix. The following is a broad overview of the YPAR and feminist methods that underpinned my multiyear study. Although these notes are specific to the project outlined in this book, I hope this appendix serves as a theoretical springboard for other educators to learn from the students in their own schools and communities.

Participatory Action Research (PAR)

Participatory action research (PAR) is a qualitative methodology that seeks to provide an alternative and empowering forum for conducting research with communities (Taylor et al., 2006). PAR projects seek to address practical problems or issues in communities (Heron & Reason, 2001). Although the particulars of each PAR project are unique, there are a number of underlying tenets that inform participatory action work, includ-

185

ing a cyclical process of: investigating a problem or issue, engaging individual and community reflection, taking action to benefit both communities and the people involved in the research project, and building cooperative alliances between coresearchers (McIntyre, 2008).

The participant-to-researcher relationship is an important difference between participatory and traditional research methods. Within participatory research, "community groups and/or community members [form] an egalitarian partnership with researchers" (Taylor et al., 2006, p. 4). YPAR projects embody all of these ideologies, and the "Y" signals that they do so with youth communities. PAR projects adopt a "strengths-based approach" toward communities, community researchers, and, in the case of YPAR, young people (Taylor et al., 2006 p. 5). Throughout the process(es), the research team becomes a unique knowledge-making community with its own relationships, objectives, and sensemaking systems. Central to PAR is a belief that not only are community members capable of research and action, but they are also, in fact, the best suited individuals to report on the status of *their* community (Heron & Reason, 2002). Further, they are often also the most effective agents to elicit change within those communities (Heron & Reason, 2002; McIntyre, 2008).

Feminist Methodologies

This project was guided and informed by feminist epistemologies (Kolmar & Barthkowski, 1999) that are committed to social change (Collins, 2000; Reinharz, 1992), recognize diversity (Collins, 2000; Reinharz, 1992), humanize researcher-participant relationships (Appadurai, 2006; Tuck, 2009), and draw on personal or lived experiences (Adichie, 2015; Hesse-Biber, 2012; hooks, 2000; Reinharz, 1992). Feminist methodologies seek to create new meanings through questioning, dialoguing, and placing the personal experiences of women at the center of social inquiry (Belenky et al., 1997; Hesse-Biber, 2012; Reinharz, 1992). Our project used personal storytelling as a vehicle to build community while learning more deeply about the lived experiences and social-emotional needs of the student researchers. Feminist researchers and activists seek to form and support caring communities to work for social change. This project was consistent with hooks's (2000) conceptualization of feminist sisterhood:

We understood that political solidarity between females expressed in sisterhood goes beyond positive recognition of the experiences of women and even shared sympathy for common suffering. Feminist sisterhood is rooted in shared commitment to struggle against patriarchal injustice, no matter the form the injustice takes. (p. 15)

During the course of this study, our community evolved into a compassionate support system. We shared compelling personal stories and built relationships with one another. However, our solidarity came not just from caring about and for each other, but also from taking action together to end mental health stigma, unmask the affective crisis, and to speak out against gender discrimination. In this way, our personal storytelling became a community platform for taking action.

Although all of the coresearchers in this project were academically high-achieving women, our diversity of perspectives, experiences, and social identities added complexity and depth to our research. We were athletes (varsity and recreational) and scholars. Members of our team identified as Republican, Democrat, Christian, Jewish, atheist, gay, straight, Vietnamese, White, Chinese, Black, and a variety of other salient identities. Within our project we explored how social identities interacted with our identification as high-achieving women. We used this understanding to then take action to better safeguard the affective needs of academically high-achieving young women.

Common Commitments: PAR and Feminist Methods

(Y)PAR is an iterative process that engages the complex personhood of individuals and communities (Appadurai, 2006). Although not explicitly feminist, the process of (Y)PAR aligns with many tenets of feminist research methods. Both research methods emphasize personal, lived experiences (Heron & Reason, 2002; hooks, 2000; Morrell, 2004) and include efforts to mitigate power dynamics between participants and facilitators/investigators. Through coresearch, participants and facilitators join together as sensemakers, learning collaboratively through cycles of observing, acting, and reflecting (James, Milenkiewicz, & Bucknam, 2008).

Although there are significant and common trends among the affective needs of high-achieving young women (Kerr, 1994; Lovecky, 2011; Maurer, 2011; Rimm 1999), our research team did not intend to provide a single generalized narrative for *all* high-achieving young women in the transition from high school to college. In fact, both PAR and feminist methods (Adichie, 2014; Brown, 2012; Collins, 1998, 2000; Kolmar & Barthkowski, 1999) aim to produce new knowledge that counters a single generalized story. If I were to do this same project with 20 different high-achieving women, I would anticipate some similar themes, as well as some departures and nuances unique to the discussions, projects, and narratives of this new group. Our project aimed for a deep exploration of the personal narratives of these specific research teams rather than a broad exploration of all high-achieving young women. In analyzing the particularities of these narratives, we gained insight into the lived experiences and social-emotional needs of high-achieving young women during the transition from high school to college.

PAR and feminist projects offer a counterhegemonic alternative to "damage-centered research" (Tuck, 2009, p. 409), which often presents marginalized communities as broken. These traditions reinforce and exacerbate hegemonic power dynamics, including teacher-student and researcher-community dynamics (Appadurai, 2006; Tuck, 2009). Conversely, PAR work aims to engage in "desire-based frameworks [that] . . . are concerned with understanding complexities, contradiction, and the self-determination of lived lives" (Tuck, 2009, p. 416). This means, to the greatest extent possible, I had to let go of constructs in which I was privileged as a "constructed knower" and the students were positioned as more disadvantaged knowers (Belenky, et al., 1997). Appadurai (2006) contended that research is a right, not to be reserved only for those with advanced degrees, but for all people as a method to investigate and make meaning of our own lived conditions, experiences, and opportunities for change.

This research project hinged on students' perceptions of their lived experiences and challenges in the high-stakes and high-stress school contexts. I believe this pursuit was only possible through learning from students in their own voices (Belenky et al., 1997). We used YPAR and feminist methodologies to mitigate the power dynamics of traditional research, produce community knowledge, and take action on issues that mattered to our research teams. The student research teams named their own affective needs and experiences. We then used this information to understand how affective education might be operationalized in schools, particularly in programs that serve high-achieving and gifted students. The students were active coresearchers in shaping the scope of this project. They led discussions (online and face-to-face), analyzed data, posed questions, and made decisions about the ways our work was shared and storied.

As coresearchers, our context, communities, and personal constraints shaped the infrastructure of our group. Although we were all fully committed to this project, I was sympathetic to the need to create meaning-making processes that were practical, humanizing, and flexible enough for the student researchers who were also busy with school, athletics, work, and extracurricular activities. The student researchers chose which aspects of the project to participate in, how fully they wanted (or were able) to participate, and their own timelines for completing project tasks. Some student researchers chose to only actively participate during their high school years, while others stayed on to continue investigating these themes throughout their college experiences.

Action

PAR projects aim to take action on practical problems or issues in communities (Heron & Reason, 2002; McIntyre, 2008). They are grounded in *doing*. As Maguire (1987) wrote, "By linking the creation of knowledge about social reality with concrete action, participatory research removes the traditional separation between knowing and doing" (p. 3). Our research team took action in distinct ways: presenting formal presentations at a prestigious governor's school for gifted youth, recording public radio stories, creating personal action plans to promote personal health and wellness, hosting a community art show on mental health, and initiating individual action projects inspired by our work together.

As a research team, we planned these events to open up dialogue around the importance of self-care for high-achieving young women in schools. The student researchers wanted to give specific strategies for self-care while also unmasking the affective crisis through courageous storytelling.

Facilitator Role

Although we designed a collaborative, feminist, participatory research project, there was still considerable leadership that I took on to shape our

189

project. This role included meetings with my committee at the university, the Institutional Review Board (IRB), and the school district research approval team. I made arrangements with our NPR member station for the radio storytelling project. I suggested scholars whose work would support our project and purchased several books for our team to review and discuss. I made arrangements for the student researchers to lead their workshops at the governor's school. With each new research team, I helped establish norms and arranged the team meetings. I wrote journal prompts for the students to consider. Frequently, I made suggestions and observations, mediated conversations, and gave guidance as requested. With input from the student researchers, I authored the chapters of this book. I know that my positionality colors much of this narrative and that if a student researcher were writing her own account of our project, her retelling would be different from my own.

In addition to being a teacher and counselor, I am nearly 20 years older than the student researchers. As such there were some boundaries inherent in our relationship. These were mostly boundaries of respect and were usually unspoken. For example, the student researchers still call me by my last name, although I signed my analytic memos and other correspondence with my initials. Although we intentionally engaged in fun team-building activities (such as aerial yoga and kickboxing classes), I was not a part of the students' social groups, nor did I attend their social events, except as a chaperone for school activities (e.g., prom) or as a guest at a graduation party. As we worked together, there were some moments when our language patterns blurred. For example, on the day of my proposal defense, Elaine sent me a text saying *#finnabeariot* (which roughly translates to *fixing to be a riot*, or *you are going to be great*).

Data Collection

This project affirmed the ubiquitous nature of data in our communities. The opportunities for learning, storytelling, understanding, and connecting are limitless. Our data collection processes centered specifically on personal story sharing. We strove for Belenky et al.'s (1997) concept of "constructed knowing" (p. 134) by reclaiming and integrating personal and public knowledge through storytelling. Table A.1 outlines the key data collection methods used in this project.

Table A.1

Data Collection Methods Used

Individual Recorded Dialogues	I met with many of the student researchers individually for recorded dialogues. These dialogues allowed me to explore the nuanced understandings and experiences that each student researcher brought to the project. The purpose of these dialogues was for the student researchers to reflect on how their hopes, fears, and perspectives on feminism and identity evolved or stayed constant throughout our project. I used a semistructured protocol, and the dialogues averaged 75 minutes in length. Although most of the student researchers wrote extensively in the reflective journals (outlined later in this table), our face-to-face, one-on-one dialogues opened up a more personal real-time format for conversation and relationship building that we all found valuable.
Team Dialogues	We met as a research team 1–3 times a week. I prepared agendas to guide our meetings, and the student researchers used (and sometimes modified) these agendas as they led the meetings. During our meetings we shared reflections and experiences, including our hopes and fears. We workshopped radio stories and planned our action projects. We also usually ate together; I believe the proverbial act of breaking bread (or bagels or Vietnamese spring rolls) together helped us form a community. As a team, we read widely on feminism (Adichie, 2014; Collins, 2000; hooks, 2000; Lorde, 1984), wholehearted living (Brown, 2010, 2012), and growth mindset (Dweck, 2006; Mohr, 2014). We used these readings and others to ground our understanding of the social-emotional needs of high-achieving young women and to buttress our arguments and action work around affective education. Our group dialogues were captured through a combination of audio recording and rich note-taking so that we could refer back to them as needed. There were times when these notes or recordings helped us remember how our conversations had unfolded. If at any time one of the student researchers asked that the recorder be turned off, I honored that request immediately. Although I hadn't anticipated it before the project, our group text message, e-mails, and other messages also became part of the data we considered in this project.
Radio Storytelling	Through radio story sharing, our research team hoped to open up a community dialogue around identity, intersectionality, social-emotional health, and feminism as explored and understood by high-achieving young women. Through a partnership with our local NPR member station, one of the student research teams practiced courageous storytelling through producing a radio piece with the guidance and support of two college women mentors (Kelsey and Michaela) from the journalism school at the local university. The student researchers had full ownership and authorship of their stories.

Table A.1, *continued*

Radio Storytelling, *continued*	Their stories focused on a self-selected facet of our project that was personally important to them (e.g., cultural identity, feminism, eating disorders, social-emotional needs, and women in STEM). These stories bridged storytelling and action work. These stories reached a broad listening base (more than 2,000 listeners or engagements to date) and are also hosted on a website where they are globally accessible.
Art Images	One of the research teams used the visual arts to explore complex themes salient to their own coming-of-age experiences, including mental health, relationships, well-being, and identity. Students used multiple mediums to express, explore, and illustrate their personal stories. Our YPAR team then analyzed and coded these art images the same way we did written text and recorded dialogues.
Reflective Journals	Through our reflective journals, we used writing as an inquiry tool. The student researchers had access to two journals. This first reflective journal was a community journal that we could all access to share thoughts and continue conversations with the whole team. The second reflective journal was a two-way journal between the individual student researcher and me. Some of the student researchers already engaged in personal journaling, and chose to also share excerpts of those entries as part of our two-way journals. I updated the two-way journals and collective journals regularly with new open-ended prompts around college decision making, feminism, identity, and social-emotional well-being. Our journals became a rich and important philosophical space for us to venture new ideas (Elliott, 1991). We all benefited from the processing time that the journals provided, particularly during our intense research schedule. Most of the student researchers were active writers in the journals. Some of the student researchers authored more than 60 single-spaced pages of text during the course of our project.
Facilitator Journal	I took diligent, reflective notes in a field journal (Creswell & Miller, 2000). By also using writing as a personal inquiry tool, I reflected on important "research moments," such as conversations I had with the student researchers, critical moments, new ideas, questions, and connections between our conversations and the literature. I found myself using my journal to reflect on my own feelings, philosophical quandaries, and reactions to things that happened during the course of our study. For instance, one conversation I had with Leslie prompted me to reflect on my own relationship with my best friend from my senior year of high school. My journal also included direct quotes from student researchers, particularly when they made me or the whole group think in new ways about affective education, wholehearted living, or the transition from high school to college.

Students as Researchers

I implicitly trusted the student researchers' thinking as valid and essential to this project. Further, throughout this project there were frequent times when the student researchers served as teachers to me. As critical researchers, the students actively engaged in the production of new knowledge around affective education, social-emotional health, and gender inequality. Our commitments to storytelling and vulnerability actively blurred boundaries and reconstructed relationships around collective meaning-making (Collins, 2000, 2013; Heron & Reason, 2002; hooks, 2000; Maguire, 1987; McIntyre, 2008).

Each student researcher brought a unique viewpoint and specialized interest to our broader themes. For instance, Faith was committed to exploring supports for young women working through disordered eating, whereas Jessica hoped to explore economic inequality and the emotional toll of the college applications process. As the students planned their action projects, they also engaged in research and learning about how to "go public" with their findings. The student researchers wanted to be sure that they were producing high-quality, academic work. For example, the students who participated in radio storytelling interviewed community experts for their stories. Although I was available for support, the student researchers had agency over these stories and projects. The following is an e-mail Leslie sent to set up an interview for her story on gender and education.

E-MAIL FROM LESLIE TO HIGHER EDUCATION PROFESSOR

May 4, 2015

Dear Dr. H.,

Hello, my name is Leslie T. and I am a member of Mrs. Fishman-Weaver's YPAR team. First, I'd like to thank you for agreeing to let me interview you for my [radio] story! I know Mrs. Fishman-Weaver sent you an email giving the basic overview of my radio piece, but I'd love to give you a little bit more information. I chose to investigate the relationship between gender, academic achievement, and professional success because I am both passionate about feminism and education. After talking with Mrs. Fishman-Weaver and doing some outside research, it became clear that women outperform men in terms of GPA across the high school, undergraduate, and graduate levels. Women are not, however, holding the highest leadership and professional positions (e.g. only 33 of the 1,000 Fortune companies are headed by women as CEOs). Thus, I wanted to discuss this in my radio piece, as it is a story that I want to tell. I think at this point the story is aiming for awareness and advocacy.

In our interview (which will only last as long as you would like it to) I will ask you some questions about what you do, where you work, etc. Then, I will open the floor for you to talk about what you think is relevant. I have looked at several of your articles online and they seem to fit perfectly with the theme of my story. In other words, you are the expert so you can talk about what you know and are passionate about. (I may come with some other specific questions, if I think of them as my story develops).

Thank you so much for agreeing to meet with me. Your opinion will be invaluable! In terms of scheduling the actual interview time, my deadline for having the recording is May 20, but I would love to meet before then. Are you free anytime this week or next week, preferably in the afternoon?

Once again, thank you! Please feel free to express any of your worries or concerns to me.

Sincerely,
Leslie T.

As a YPAR project facilitator, I mentored the students in becoming critical researchers (Morrell, 2004). For the most part, the students were only familiar with the positivist, quantitative methods learned in their science classes and observed at their STEM internships. Leslie was an exception, having done some qualitative work in her internship.

Data Analysis

The student researchers had a preference for road maps, algorithms, and finding "right" answers, so we started with a bit more structure than I might have, had I orchestrated an individual project. Drawing on their background from our empowerment group, we identified three primary tensions to explore. These tensions were (1) self-care and self-harm, (2) vulnerability and guardedness, (3) strength and limitation.

To break down the data each week for our analytic memos, I used these tensions as sensitizing concepts (Charmaz, 2014). However, I also read more broadly for emerging themes, points of contention, and points of salience that we might not have considered (Charmaz, 2014). Once a week, I read through the student researchers' individual and collective journals, my own field journal, our group text messages and any other texts the student researchers had shared with me (e.g., essays and e-mails). Additionally, we took many photos during this project. Although the photos were not used as a data, I found it helpful to look back on this visual representation of our story as I read the texts. As I read and reread the story of our data process from each week, I put together an analytic memo in letter form to the student researchers that outlined and gave examples of key themes and concepts across our data. These also included instances when we disagreed or had different experiences. The first draft of each analytic memo offered my personal reading of our work. However, I posted these memos to our collaborative online repository, where the student researchers were actively encouraged to comment, critique, and add to them. Thus, the analytic memos were living documents throughout the project.

We employed a cyclical and participatory analytic process through collaborative analytic memos (Heron & Reason, 2002; Maguire, 1987; McIntyre, 2008). Although I was committed to a participatory process, I also recognized that research with communities needs to employ a pragmatism that honors the lives of individuals (Appadurai, 2006). For us, the student researchers' high stress and very full schedules were real material limitations that I wanted to respect. Therefore, our analytic memos enabled me to take on the time-heavy pieces of analysis, including reading and rereading all texts and transcribing dialogues. The students then responded to these memos with their own reflections, modifications, and interpretations.

As the first step in our analytic process, these analytic memos directly contributed to and supported our iterative and cyclical processes (Heron & Reason, 2002; Maguire, 1987; McIntyre, 2008). The student researchers and I came back to analytic memos from previous weeks with new knowledge and added new reflections and questions to the concepts, themes, and tensions we had seen or experienced. If there was a concept that I noticed several of us were wrestling with, I added it to our other research activities for the following week, either by writing a journal prompt that pushed our thinking on that subject, finding a relevant reading, or adding it as a conversation topic for an upcoming team meeting. Often our experiences led to new reflections on these concepts, which led to us taking action; this was a process that we reflected on in our individual writings and dialogues, and then as a team. For example, one week we spent a lot of time talking about the importance of peer groups and friend relationships. A student researcher then commented that she sometimes felt as if her peers were offering "false support." This new concept of false support caused the student researchers to reexamine their friendships, relationships, and peer groups. The students wrote examples and reflections about this concept in their team journal, and we then discussed relationships with a new level of complexity at our next team meeting. Through this iterative and cyclical process, our research team had multiple opportunities and ways to engage and reflect on the concepts, tensions, and themes we identified as important.

Our analytic process continued during our weekly meetings as we reflected on our collective responses to the analytic memos and discussed points of contention, intersection, unrest, and salience. These discussions continued to push the themes in new directions. For example, through our varied discussions, writings, readings, and experiences, we came to more nuanced understandings of strength, gender, emotion, vulnerability, and courage. As we came to these new understandings, we attempted to operationalize them in both our personal lives and groups meetings (e.g., practicing deep breathing and sharing courageous stories). Once we had done this, we used this new knowledge to take action to support more young women in our communities (e.g., leading a workshop on deep breathing and sharing our courageous stories publically). In this way, we moved from information to personal reflection, to group dialogue, to public action, which then prompted us to seek more information, reflection, and dialogue—thus marrying our data collection and analysis processes.

All of our data collection activities were language-rich and were in themselves opportunities for analysis and the production of knowledge (St. Pierre, 2000). Feminist researchers (e.g. Butler, 2006; St. Pierre, 2000) wrote that all dialogues and reflections are inherently both data collection and data analysis. I wanted to put our dialogues and reflections in conversation with each other. In addition to what we discovered about the lived experiences and social-emotional needs of high-achieving young women, we also learned a tremendous amount from becoming a critical, feminist research team.

Member Checks

In qualitative work, member checking is "the most crucial technique for establishing credibility" (Lincoln & Guba, 1985, p. 314). Participatory work, which depends on collective inquiry and sensemaking, is not possible without member checking (McIntyre, 2008). To ensure that member checking and individual voices were a regular part of our research process, I scheduled regular member-check conversations with the student researchers. These conversations served as a reciprocal and cyclical evaluation of our data and project. This process also supported our team's commitment to cocreating meaning. In addition to checking for understanding, these conversations were a standing opportunity for the student researchers and me to connect one-on-one to discuss the research project. Additionally, the student researchers read and critiqued chapter and section drafts and gave me feedback on those. I incorporated this feedback and shared subsequent drafts to make sure I was representing the thinking of our research team accurately.

Peer Checks

The student researchers and I sought feedback from several of our peers, some of whom are mentioned throughout this book. In these conversations, we asked for feedback on our analysis, findings, recommendations, and action projects. Our peer groups gave us generous feedback, pushback, and reflections on the ways we conceptualized the problem of the study, our analytical frames, analysis, and implications (Creswell & Miller, 2000; Lincoln & Guba, 1985). Throughout the writing of this study, I sought the peer feedback of alumnae from our first empowerment group, as well as feedback of women educators and researchers who also worked with gifted youth. These peers challenged and pushed me in ways that made my thinking deeper and my writing stronger (Creswell & Miller, 2000).

Ethics and Reflexivity

Ethics and reflexivity are inexorably linked in qualitative research projects and in YPAR work in particular (Marshall & Rossman, 2014). Positionality, reflexivity, and ethics were themes that ran throughout these strands of investigation, education, and research (Guillemin & Gillam, 2004; Maguire, 1987). Cannella and Lincoln (2011) wrote, "critical, radical ethics is relational and collaborative; it aligns with resistance and marginality" (p. 81). My preestablished rapport with the student researchers gave me great insight into the nuances of our discussions. Our existing and caring relationship allowed the students to open up more quickly, and as Marshall and Rossman (2014) would argue, *more honestly*, to me than they would with a stranger. I was a frequent confidant as these women navigated coming-of-age and the transition from high school to college. This closeness gave us rich narratives and contributed to very personal disclosure. Such disclosure falls under a category of everyday microethics (Guillemin & Gillam, 2004). As a YPAR researcher, I constantly navigated these ethically important, albeit small, moments.

In ethical jargon, the principle of beneficence guided my work. This required that my research and actions were intended to benefit others (Guillemin & Gillam, 2004). In particular, I was committed to acting in ways that benefited the student research team and its goals in making a difference for other gifted youth. I worked in partnership with our comprehensive guidance department to safeguard the social-emotional well-being of the student researchers. As mentioned earlier, some of the student researchers were working through complex and challenging social-emotional struggles.

A Kantian maxim states that "people should never be used merely as a means to someone else's end" (Guillemin & Gillam, 2004 p. 271). I chose a YPAR, feminist research framework for its insistence that "the outcome of good research is not just books or academic papers, but it is also the creative action of people to address issues that are important to them" (Heron & Reason, 2001, p. 179). From the beginning of the project, the student researchers and I discussed how we wanted our work to be used to make a positive difference for real issues we collectively cared about. Ultimately, we hoped to support high-achieving young women lead healthier, more balanced lives.

IRB and School District Approval

The local university Institutional Review Board (IRB) approved this project. I had IRB-approved written consent forms (for students 18 and older) and parent consent/child assent forms (for students under 18). Our study posed minimal risk to the student researchers. I informed the students that their participation, including their levels of participation, was voluntary. The student researchers were told they could stop participating at any point. Additionally, we talked through a range of ways to participate in this research project, including scaling back and opting out if needed.

The school district I worked with also had a separate research approval process. I detailed our research study processes with the school district's research approval team. Additionally, because this study addressed social-emotional concerns, I shared information about the specific students I was working with so that we could determine if any of the potential student researchers were too psychologically fragile to participate. The school district agreed with the IRB that our study posed minimal risk and that all of the necessary protections were in place for us to conduct our study. In fact, both the university IRB and the school district commented that our study might have personal benefits to the student researchers in allowing them to process their own experiences and needs with a peer group and trained facilitators.

Student Well-Being

Beyond the research protections required by the IRB, or even the school district research approval team, I wanted to be certain that I had a plan in place should any of our work trigger difficult emotions for the student researchers. I had an established relationship with our guidance department and worked closely with the counselors at Barnwood to address the more intense social-emotional needs of some of the young women on our research teams. As a mandated reporter, I was also required to work with school personnel if instances of abuse or extreme harm/self-harm came up at any time during our project. As needed, I worked with our guidance and crisis personnel immediately, regardless of any impacts this intervention might have on our study. My values as a researcher began by honoring students; therefore, safeguarding well-being was my steady moral compass throughout this project.

About the Author

Kathryn Fishman-Weaver, Ph.D., is an educator, author, and advocate for student leadership. She has a group of exceptional students in Oakland, CA, to thank for teaching her how to be a teacher. Dr. Fishman-Weaver has gone on to use these lessons to work in special education, gifted education, English language arts, and teacher preparation. Currently she serves as the Director of Academic Affairs and Engagement for Mizzou K–12 where she learns with students and teachers across the globe. Dr. Fishman-Weaver writes and presents frequently on student support, teacher leadership, and gender and education. She loves the written word, a good nap, and impromptu family dance parties in her kitchen.